Embracing the Light

Reflections on God's Word

To Sally,
with fond memories
of our years at Carleton,

Mary

June 2016

Embracing the Light

Reflections on God's Word

by Mary Nelson Keithahn

LILJA
PRESS

Copyright © 2016 by Mary Keithahn

Design by Lilja Press

Published by Lilja Press
8953 Aztec Drive, Eden Prairie, Minnesota 55347

www.liljapress.com

Library of Congress Cataloging-in-Publication Data

Keithahn, Mary N.
Embracing the Light
Reflections on God's Word/Mary Nelson Keithahn
ISBN: 978-0-9843742-5-0
Library of Congress Control Number: 2016940281
Printed in the United States of America
First printing June 2016

*With gratitude to God, whose voice is never silent,
and to all those, past and present, who in different ways
have given me new insights into the light and truth
that continue to emanate from God's Holy Word.*

Preface

The unfolding of your words gives light; it imparts understanding to the simple. (Psalm 119:130)

When the little group of Separatist Pilgrims started out from Holland for the New World in 1620, their beloved pastor, John Robinson, stayed behind to care for the majority of his flock that remained in Leyden. Robinson was a confirmed Calvinist who never wavered from his biblical faith, yet he did not consider the Bible a closed book. His willingness to be open to new inspirations and insights from God's Holy Word was reflected in his farewell address to the Pilgrims (emphasis mine):

> I charge you...that you follow me no farther than you have seen me follow the Lord Jesus Christ. If God reveal anything to you, by any other instrument of his, be as ready to receive it as ever you were to receive any truth by my ministry: for I am verily persuaded *the Lord has more truth yet to break forth out of his holy Word.* For my part, I cannot sufficiently bewail the condition of the Reformed churches, who are come to a period in religion, and will go at present no farther than the instruments of their reformation. The Lutherans cannot be drawn to go beyond what Luther saw; whatever part of his will our God has revealed to Calvin, they will rather die than embrace it; and the Calvinists, you see, stick fast where they were left by that great man of God, who yet saw not all things. This is a misery much to be lamented, for though they were burning and shining lights in their times, yet they penetrated not into the whole counsel of God, but were they now living, would be as *willing to embrace farther light* as that which they first received. I beseech you remember, it is an article of your church-covenant, that you be ready to receive whatever truth shall be made known to you from the written Word of God.

As a life-long member of a Christian denomination that traces its roots back to the Separatists who landed in Plymouth in 1620, I have always considered myself one of their spiritual descendants. (Recently I have discovered I am also a biological descendant of eight of their number!) Like John Robinson, my faith is based on the Bible I love, but I too believe that God continues to speak to us through its words, ever enlightening us with a new understanding of the world around and beyond us, and our role as followers of Jesus. Rather than fear these new insights, I embrace them as a means to grow and act on my faith. I can sing wholeheartedly these words of George Rawson from our hymnal:

> *We limit not the truth of God to our poor reach of mind,*
> *to notions of our day and place, crude, partial, and confined.*
> *No, let a new and better hope within our hearts be stirred,*
> *Oh, God, grant yet more light and truth to break forth*
> *from your word.*[1]

Over the years of what has become a very long life, I have often reflected on the new insights and understanding that I have gained by looking at my life and the world around me through the lens of the Bible. These meditations have resulted from these thoughts. May they help you see and embrace the light and truth that breaks forth from God's Holy Word in your lives as well.

Mary Nelson Keithahn

1. *George Rawson, 1853, alt. The entire hymn is included in the* New Century Hymnal *(Cleveland: Pilgrim Press, 1995). The text has been slightly altered for inclusive and archaic language.*

Table of Contents

Creator, Christ, and Holy Spirit

GOD

Christian Year

Other Special Days and Seasons

Christian Life

CHURCH

FAITH

FACING DEATH

CARING FOR ONE ANOTHER

REPENTANCE AND FORGIVENESS

MISSION

CREATOR, CHRIST, AND HOLY SPIRIT

Embracing the Light

Picture God

No one has ever seen God. (1 John 4:12a[1])

If someone asked you to draw a picture of God, what would the picture be like?

> A benevolent, bearded, white-haired man with a kind smile on his face and presents in his hands?

> A Santa Claus who's been "making a list and checking it twice" to find out "who's naughty and nice" so he can reward people accordingly?

> A CIA-type in a trenchcoat and dark glasses, lurking around the corner, ready to catch us in some wrongful act?

> A wonderful magician who defies the laws of nature to cause miracles to happen?

> A stern boss who sets rules and regulations that make impossible demands on us?

> A sculptor who creates us and then goes on to other things, leaving us to struggle alone?

Or a loving parent who loves us and stands by us no matter what happens?

I suspect that no two pictures of God would be the same.

As the son of missionary parents in India, my husband had traveled across the ocean several times by ship. He loved the sea in all its vastness and infinite variety of moods. He was very much aware of how small a part of it could be seen from any particular point on shore, or on board ship, or even from the air. He often said that trying to know God was like trying to view the ocean all at one time. God is so great that, from our particular moment in time and space, we can only experience a tiny, tiny part of who God is. Our limited experience of God is but a fragment of the whole picture. We need to look at God through the eyes of others, too.

The Bible is a good place to start. The people of the Bible did not create visual images of the God who acted in their lives, but they used many word pictures to describe how they experienced the Holy One. These metaphors are still helpful, and encourage us to come up with new ways to describe the God we know.

Prayer: *How great you are, God, and how limited is our vision of*
           your glory! Open our eyes to see your love at work in
           our lives, we pray. Amen.

1. *All scripture verses are taken from the New Revised Standard Version of the Bible, unless otherwise noted.*

God Is My Fortress

The Lord is my rock, my fortress, and my deliverer, my God, my rock in whom I take refuge. (Psalm 18:2a)

The psalmist's picture of God as a stone fortress offering protection from all harm made more sense to me after a trip to Germany and Austria. Wherever we went, castles loomed up on the horizon, many dating back to the Late Middle Ages. When we took a boat up the Rhine River, we could see fortified castles built on the rocky heights above the water all along the way. We got off at one port and hiked up the long, winding road to the ruins of Burg Rheinfels. Here, 300 years ago, a force of four thousand Germans successfully withstood an attack from a French army of 28,000. Inside the moats and thick walls of Burg Rheinfels, there had been buildings used as bedrooms, a great hall, a kitchen, offices, an arsenal, storage rooms, various work rooms, and a chapel. The inner courtyards had space for kitchen gardens, as well as a place of safety for villagers from nearby St. Goar in case of attack.

Built on solid rock high above the river, heavily fortified, and completely self-sufficient, Burg Rheinfels was indeed a "fortress" and a "refuge" for people in that area. Standing inside that castle, I understood why Martin Luther wrote in his great hymn,

A mighty fortress is our God, a bulwark never failing;
Our helper he amid the flood of mortal ills prevailing.[1]

Martin Luther's use of "a mighty fortress" as a metaphor for the protective, life-saving, nurturing love of God was indeed appropriate. After all, had he not found a refuge in Castle Wartburg, a similar fortress, when he was fleeing from persecution for his religious beliefs? And within that refuge a strong foundation for his faith?

Prayer: *God, our hope and our strength, shelter us from the storms*
          of life within the fortress of your love. Amen.

---

1. *Martin Luther, c. 1529. The entire hymn is included in* The United Methodist Hymnal *(The United Methodist Publishing House, 1989).*

A Mother Eagle and a Potter

As an eagle stirs up its nest, and hovers over its young; as it spreads its wings, takes them up, and bears them aloft on its pinions, the Lord alone guided him. (Deuteronomy 32:11-12a)

"He [the potter] was working at his wheel. The vessel he was making of clay was spoiled in the potter's hand, and he reworked it into another vessel, as seemed good to him." (Jeremiah 18:3-4)

The Book of Deuteronomy pictures God as caring for Israel "like an eagle hovering over its nest, overshadowing its young, then spreading its wings, lifting them into the air, teaching them to fly."[1] Mother and father eagles are thought to care for their young together, teaching them to fly by carrying them on their wings high into a draft of air, dropping them into the current, and then swooping below them to catch them again on their wings as they tire or flounder. What a beautiful picture this is of God as a supportive Teacher who enables us to use our abilities to develop new skills!

But what happens when we fail to learn? What happens when we don't succeed at the tasks God gives us? Jeremiah offers an answer in his picture of God as a potter. If a pot that the potter creates out of clay turns out to be imperfect, the potter can take that clay and re-work it into something new and better. God can do the same with us. Adelaide Pollard used this metaphor in her hymn:

Have thine own way, Lord! Have thine own way!
Thou art the Potter, I am the clay.
Mold me and make me after thy will,
while I am waiting, yielded and still. [2]

Isn't it wonderful that we can count on God to show us how to be the persons we were created to be, to forgive us when we fail, and to offer us another chance to fulfill our purpose?

Prayer: *Thank you, God, for helping us learn and grow, and being there for us when we falter and fail. Thank you too for second chances and new beginnings. Amen.*

---

1. The Message: The Bible in Contemporary Language, *by Eugene H. Peterson. Copyright © 2002 by Eugene H. Peterson. All rights reserved.*

2. Adelaide A. Pollard, 1902. The entire hymn is included in The United Methodist Hymnal *(The United Methodist Publishing House, 1989).*

Embracing the Light

God Unlimited

But you, O Lord, are a God merciful and gracious, slow to anger and abounding in steadfast love and faithfulness. (Psalm 86:15)

When I was growing up in Minnesota, my family had a summer cottage on Lake Koronis. From our shore, we could see the cabins and boathouses on the other side of the lake. We often got into our boat and rowed over to that shore and around the lake. We knew that body of water thoroughly: how large it was, where the stream was that fed it, where the dam was that held the water in the lake, where the water was deep and where it was shallow.

Our human capacity for love is like that lake: predictable, limited by circumstances, sometimes shallow, sometimes deep. The love of God, however, is like the ocean, so great that we cannot measure it from our limited perspective. We cannot see its boundaries, or sound its depths from where we stand. God's love is too great to comprehend, too wise, too forgiving, too enabling for us to measure by our human standards. Hymn writer Frederick Faber put it this way:

> *There's a wideness in God's mercy,*
> *like the wideness of the sea;*
> *there's a kindness in his justice,*
> *which is more than liberty.*

There's no place where earthly sorrows
are more felt than in God's heaven;
there's no place where earthly failings
have such kindly judgment given.

For the love of God is broader
than the measures of our mind;
and the heart of the Eternal
is most wonderfully kind.

If our love were but more faithful,
we would gladly trust God's word;
and our lives would show thanksgiving
for the goodness of our Lord.[1]

Prayer: *Help us always remember, God, that our definitions of*
your mercy can never limit the width and breadth and depth
of your love. Amen.

---

1. *Frederick William Faber, 1854, alt. The hymn is included in the* New Century Hymnal *(Cleveland: Pilgrim Press, 1995).*

Embracing the Light

It Takes A Whole Village…
to Know God

God arranged the members in the body, each one of them, as he chose. If all were a single member, where would the body be? As it is, there are many members, yet one body. The eye cannot say to the hand, "I have no need of you," nor again the head to the feet, "I have no need of you."…If one member suffers, all suffer together with it; if one member is honored, all rejoice together with it. (1 Corinthians 12:18-21, 26)

Once upon a time in India, six friends shared a home in a little village. Although not one of them could see, their other senses were keen, and they used them to help one another. They got around by holding hands and walking in a line. The first man would feel his way, and the others would follow.

One day the men heard about a great animal called an elephant. They were filled with curiosity, and couldn't wait to see it. Joining hands, they lined up behind the first man and went off to find an acquaintance that lived next door to the Rajah who owned a herd of elephants. He found them a patient elephant that stood quietly while they explored his great body with their fingers.

The first man touched the elephant's side. It felt both smooth and rough, and solid like a rock. "It's very like a wall," he said. The second man felt the elephant's tusk and drew his hand away quickly. "Oh, no," he said, "an elephant is sharp and pointed like a spear." The third man found the elephant's trunk. "Oh, my," he said in a quavering voice, "it's long and thin and coiled like a snake!" The fourth man started at the toes and worked his way up the elephant's leg. "You're wrong," he said, "this elephant is like a tree, perhaps with coconuts on the top." The fifth man felt the elephant's ear. "It's flat and wide, a leather fan." The sixth man pulled the elephant's tail, and said, "Anyone can see that an elephant is like a twisted cord, a piece of rope, a woman's braid."

The six friends started arguing. Each one had "seen" the elephant differently, and they could not agree on what it was. The elephant's owner heard their shouting and hurried over to rescue his animal. "Foolish men," he said, "you are all right. You have each 'seen' part of my elephant. Put your ideas together and you'll have a complete picture."

And that's just what they did. "An elephant is an elephant, and we have each seen it in our own way. Now we can go home." Lining up again, hand in hand, behind the first man, they followed him as he felt his way back to their village.[1]

Prayer: *You are like that elephant, God, too great for any one of us to know completely from our limited experience. There is more to know about you than we can each see in our own way. Help us respect the views of others and learn from them that we might gain a more complete picture of how much you love and care for us and all your children. Amen.*

1. *This ancient fable has been retold many times. Author-illustrator Ed Young used the story in his delightful picture book,* Seven Blind Mice, *which won the Caldecott Medal (Philomel Books, 1992).*

Embracing the Light

One God, Many Names

Hear, O Israel: The Lord is our God, the Lord alone.
(Deuteronomy 6:4)

*A wandering Aramean was my ancestor; he went down into Egypt
and lived there as an alien, few in number, and there he became a great
nation, mighty and populous. When the Egyptians treated us harshly
and afflicted us, by imposing hard labor on us, we cried to the Lord, the
God of our ancestors; the Lord heard our voice and saw our affliction,
our toil, and our oppression. The Lord brought us out of Egypt with
a mighty hand and an outstretched arm, with a terrifying display of
power, and with signs and wonders; and he brought us into this place
and gave us this land, a land flowing with milk and honey.*
(Deuteronomy 26:5b-9)

*Lord, you have been our dwelling place in all generations. Before the
mountains were brought forth, or ever you had formed the earth and
the world, from everlasting to everlasting you are God.* (Psalm 90:1-2)

When our oldest child was learning to talk, he would often point
to objects and ask, "What's that?" It was no surprise to us then
that he asked the same question the first time he saw his baby
sister! She was another new part of his world. As he got to know
her, she became a "who" instead of a "what," and his names for her
expanded: little sister, playmate, rival, friend.

We may learn the given names of people when we are introduced
to them, but it is only as we come to know them through shared

experiences that we begin to identify them by other names: partner, mentor, colleague, friend. So it is with God. As we experience the divine presence in our lives, we choose names for God that are meaningful to us and add new names to the list. It was the Hebrew people's experiences with God in Egypt, in the wilderness, and in the Promised Land that led them to proclaim: "God is one, not many. God hears our cries and answers them. God is eternal, without beginning or end."

Many centuries later, in the Black Hills of South Dakota, a Lakota medicine man and mystic named Black Elk used words from his tribal language to affirm the same qualities in God. He called God "Tunkashila" and "Wakantanka." Tunkashila is the Lakota word for "Grandfather." Wakan means "mysterious and holy" and Tanka means "great." For Black Elk, God was the "Great Spirit" who was like a wise and compassionate grandfather to all creatures and creation. Thus he prayed:

> *Grandfather, Great Spirit, you have always been and before you no one has been. There is no other one to pray to but you. You yourself, everything that you see, has been made by you. The star nation all over the universe you have finished. The four quarters of the earth you have finished. Grandfather, Great Spirit, lean close to the earth that you may hear the voice I send….Give me the strength to walk the soft earth, a relative to all that is! Give me the eyes to see and the strength to understand, that I may be like you. With your power only can I face the winds.*[1]

Prayer: *May the names we give you, God, help others find meaning in your presence in our lives. Amen.*

---

1. *Excerpt from* Black Elk Speaks, *by John G. Niehardt (State University of New York Press, annotated edition, 2008).*

Embracing the Light

Where Love Is, There God Is Also

No one has ever seen God; if we love one another, God lives in us, and his love is perfected in us....God is love, and those who abide in love abide in God, and God abides in them. (1 John 4:12, 16b)

One of the stories on the web a few years ago was about a little boy who wanted to go see God. He knew it would be a long trip, so he filled his backpack with Twinkies and a six-pack of root beer before he set off. He had gone only three blocks when he met an old woman, sitting in the park staring sadly at some pigeons.

The little boy sat down beside the woman and opened his backpack. He thought the old woman looked hungry, so he offered her a Twinkie. She smiled at him and graciously accepted the little cake. Her smile charmed the little boy, and he offered her a root beer. To his delight, she gave him a big smile again.

The two of them sat in the park all afternoon, sharing the little boy's lunch and smiling at one another, never saying a word. It grew dark, and the little boy realized it was time to go home. He got up to leave, but then turned and gave the woman a hug. She gave him her biggest smile ever.

When the little boy opened the door of his house, his mother saw the look of joy on his face. "What made you so happy today?" she asked. The little boy replied. "I had lunch with God, and you know what? She's got the most beautiful smile!"

Meanwhile, the old woman, returned to her home, radiant with joy. Her son was amazed at the change. "Mother," he asked, "what did you do today that made you so happy?" She replied, "I ate Twinkies in the park with God." Before her son could respond, she added, "You know, he's much younger than I expected."

In a simple act of sharing, an old woman felt God's presence in the kindness of a little boy, and the little boy, in turn, saw God's love reflected in the face of an old woman who graciously accepted his gifts. For a brief time, they were bound together. Then they embraced and went their separate ways, filled with the joy of loving and being loved.

Prayer: *God, whenever we show love to one another, we know you are present among us. Guide our words and deeds that we may often be your hosts. Amen.*

Embracing the Light

Circle of Love

Before the mountains were brought forth, or ever you had formed the earth and the world, from everlasting to everlasting you are God. (Psalm 90:2)

It is not surprising that the circle has become a symbol for the eternal presence of God in many cultures from ancient times. As a set of all points that are the same distance from a given center point, a circle has no beginning or end and can be expanded to encompass all creation.

The "medicine wheel" is a traditional symbol for the Lakota people in South Dakota. The circle represents spiritual healing and wholeness, the cross inside the circle points to the four directions, and the space between the bars are the elements of fire, air, water, and earth. Traditional Lakota teepee homes were circular, they dance in a circle at their powwows, and gather in a circle for meetings and worship.

When my daughter Becky and I went with a small group to Scotland in 2005, we were surprised to learn that the Celts had also lived in circular homes and gathered in circles when they met together. Celtic Christians always placed a circle around the arms of the tall stone crosses that marked their sacred places, a practice probably coming from the "wheel cross" early Christians had used to identify themselves to one another. Within the circle that symbolized God, they would add a Greek "Chi" (like our *X*) with "Rho" (like our

P) superimposed on one of its crossbars, to represent Christ. It was a perfect symbol for the Celts, who thought of God as the center of time and space. Celtic Christians even prayed a "caim" or encircling prayer. They would stand with their right hand extended and turn clockwise, drawing an imaginary circle in the air around themselves, and then pray within this sacred place, protected by God's love: "Keep light near, and darkness afar. Keep peace within, keep harm without. Keep love within, keep hatred out."

A poem by Edwin Markham reminds us, however, that even the circle has its limitations as a symbol for God's love and care for all creation. Sometimes it separates us from one another.

> He drew a circle that shut me out—
> Heretic, rebel, a thing to flout,
> But love and I had the wit to win:
> We drew a circle and took him in![1]

It is only when the love of God radiates out from its center through the arms of Christ and its followers to encompass the whole world that the circle becomes a truly perfect symbol for the One who is from everlasting to everlasting.

Prayer: *Encircle us with your boundless love, God, and keep us in your care. May we always draw that circle wide enough to share that love with all of your creation. Amen.*

---

1. "Outwitted," from The Shoes of Happiness and Other Poems, *by Edwin Markham (Doubleday, Page & Company, 1915 paperback published 2014 by TheClassics.us).*

You Can't Run Away from God

So [Jesus] told them this parable.…"What woman having ten silver coins, if she loses one of them, does not light a lamp, sweep the house, and search carefully until she finds it? When she has found it, she calls together her friends and neighbors, saying, 'Rejoice with me, for I have found the coin that I had lost.' Just so, I tell you, there is joy in the presence of the angels of God over one sinner who repents."
(Luke 15:3, 8-10)

In Margaret Wise Brown's charming picture book, *The Runaway Bunny*,[1] a little bunny tells his mother about a number of different plans he has to run away from home. But wherever the bunny plans to go, his mother responds that she will be waiting for him there.

"If you become a fish, I will become a fisherman and fish for you," she says. "If you become a bird and fly away, I will become a tree that you can come home to."

Finally, the little bunny says with a sigh, "Shucks, I might just as well stay where I am and be your little bunny."

The little bunny had discovered what the psalmist knew:

> *Where can I go from your spirit?*
> *Or where can I flee from your presence?*
> *If I ascend to heaven, you are there;*
> *if I make my bed in Sheol, you are there.*

If I take the wings of the morning
and settle at the farthest limits of the sea,
even there your hand shall lead me,
and your right hand shall hold me fast.
(Psalm 139:7-10)

Prayer: *How wonderful it is, God, that no matter how hard we*
try to run away from you, you never run away
from us. Whether we admit it or not, we
are always in your loving care. Thank you. Amen.

---

1. The Runaway Bunny, *by Margaret Wise Brown, illustrated by Clement Hurd*
(HarperCollins, rev. edition, 2005).

Beautiful in God's Eyes

As a lily among the brambles, so is my love among maidens.
(Song of Solomon 2:2)

Becky Reyher has written a story about Varya, a little girl who lived in Russia.[1] Varya's father was a hardworking wheat farmer. At harvest time, he would cut the grain, and Varya and her mother would walk behind him to tie and stack the bundles of grain. When the day was hot, Varya would have to stop and rest. After all, she was only six years old. One day, as she lay in the shade of the next row of wheat, Varya fell asleep. When she awoke, the day was cool, and her parents were nowhere in sight. She was frightened, and ran through the fields looking for them.

Some strangers heard her cry. "What are your parents' names?" they asked. All she could say was, "My mother is the most beautiful woman in the world!" *Ah*, the strangers thought, *that will give us something to go on.* They rounded up all the beautiful women in the village, but Varya's mother was not among them. Suddenly a woman rushed toward them. She had a round, broad face, and a large body. Her eyes were slits on either side of a great nose. Her mouth was almost toothless. Varya fell into her arms, crying with joy. "Here she is," she shouted. "I told you my mother is the most beautiful woman in the world!"

Prayer: *God, we are glad you look at us the way little Varya looked*
          at her mother. Whether we are tall or short, fat or thin,
          young or old, black or white, male or female, we know we
          are beautiful in your eyes, because you love us. May we
          too always look upon one another with the eyes of love. Amen.

1. My Mother is the Most Beautiful Woman in the World, *a Russian Folk Tale*
re-told by Becky Reyher (William Morrow & Co., 1995).

Getting It Right

Do not judge by appearances, but judge with right judgment.
(John 7:24)

One spring, just before Easter, my granddaughter Katie came over with her parents to help me decorate my Easter egg tree. Katie was just three years old, and as three-year-olds are wont to do, she moved quickly from one activity to another. After we had decorated the tree, she asked for a story, played with my dog, helped me set the table for supper, and rode my exercise bike. She finally ended up in the bathroom, weighing herself on my hospital scale. After she had adjusted the balance weights to her liking, she announced with great satisfaction, "I cost 32 dollars!" Her parents and I could not help but smile as we replied, 'Yes, you weigh 32 pounds."

How like a child to confuse abstract concepts such as weight and monetary value! But are children the only ones who measure themselves wrong? I think it's a problem at every age. When we are growing up, we measure ourselves by the standards of our peers: Are we popular? Do we wear the right clothes? Are we at the top of the class? Did we make the team? We set high goals for ourselves, and when we don't measure up we become discouraged and depressed, and sometimes quit trying. We are sure no one will accept us as we are, probably because we have such a hard time accepting others as they are. We tend to judge others as harshly as we judge ourselves.

When we become adults, we set new goals: rising to the top of our profession, making lots of money, owning a beautiful home, enjoying a happy marriage, raising perfect children. But somehow, in the middle of our adult life, we have to come to terms with our life as it is. We haven't advanced in our profession. We have to struggle to make ends meet. Our first marriage ended in divorce and our second is in trouble. Our children are having problems in school. And no one looks to us at all for leadership in the community. Moreover, if we take our faith seriously, we probably know that we, like Paul, do not do the good we want to do or avoid the evil we don't want to do. How do we cope with our unfulfilled expectations and our failure to measure up to our standards?

From the stories of Elijah and Jeremiah, Peter and Paul, Zacchaeus and Mary Magdalene, and all those other unlovable, unworthy, underachieving, undistinguished human beings in the Bible, we know that God measures us on a different scale, not by who we are but by who we can become through the power of Love. And that, my friends, is cause for hope!

Prayer: *God of love, all loves excelling, no matter how unworthy we feel, you always treat us as if we were deserving of your love. Fill us with that same love, that we might measure one another, and ourselves, not by human standards but by yours. May we always act toward our neighbors in a way that makes them feel worthy in your sight and ours. Amen.*

Unconditional Love

I have loved you with an everlasting love; therefore I have continued my faithfulness to you. (Jeremiah 31:3bc)

Whenever I have a "Pauline" moment and think about the times I "do not do what I want, but I do the very thing I hate" (Romans 8:15), I marvel at the fact that God still loves and cares for me. I am comforted by Jeremiah's promise to the Hebrew people, who also had their ups and downs on the faithfulness meter.

Barbara Joosse's charming picture book set in the Arctic[1] speaks to this theme of unconditional love. A little girl asks, "Mama, do you love me?" When her mother reassures her with a hug, she asks, "How much?" Her mother replies with countless illustrations from the natural world, but then the little girl gets down to the real question. "Would you love me...if I fell and dropped all the ptarmigan eggs we had gathered? If I played some very naughty tricks on you and misbehaved badly? If I ran away to live in a cave? If I changed into a walrus or became a polar bear and chased you?" Each time the little girl's mother replied, "I would be sorry...I would be angry...I would be sad...I would be surprised and scared...but you are still you, and I will love you forever and always, because you are my dear one."

That is God's promise to us! It is also the kind of love God wants us to show to one another.

Prayer: *Faithful, loving God, you forgive us when we leave undone those things we ought to have done, and do those things we ought not to have done. Help us to respond to the failures of others with the same love and compassion we have received from you. Amen.*

---

1. Mama, Do You Love Me? *By Barbara M. Joosse, illustrated by Barbara Lavallee (Chronicle Books, 1991).*

God Measures Us Right

You judge by human standards; I judge no one. Yet even if I do judge, my judgment is valid; for it is not I alone who judge, but I and the Father who sent me. (John 8:15-16)

In her play, *A Raisin in the Sun*[1], Lorraine Hansberry writes about a family living in the projects, working and saving for the day when they can move out of their apartment into a real house and be somebody. Everyone is working toward that goal: Beneatha, her brother Walter and his wife Ruth, and Mama, who was the glue that held them all together. As they are about to realize their dream, Walter takes it upon himself to risk all the family money on a friend's get-rich-quick scheme. The friend absconds with the money, and the family is devastated, especially Beneatha. She bitterly criticizes Walter in front of Mama, who stops her short saying, "You feeling like you is better than he is today?…You done wrote his epitaph too—like the rest of the world? Well, who give you the privilege?…I thought I taught you to love him." Beneatha replies, "Love him? There's nothing left to love."

"There is always something left to love," says Mama. "And if you ain't learned that, you ain't learned nothing. Have you cried for that boy today? I don't mean for yourself and for the family 'cause we lost the money. I mean for him; what he been through and what it done to him. Child, when do you think is the time to love somebody the most: when they done good and made things easy for everybody? Well then, you ain't through learning—because that ain't the time at all. It's when he's at his lowest and can't believe in hisself 'cause the world done whipped him so. When you starts measuring somebody, measure him right, child, measure him right. Make sure you done taken into account what hills and valleys he come through before he got to where he is."

"When you starts measuring somebody, measure him right." But what is the right standard of measure? According to Mama, it is love: love that can show compassion for someone who fails, love that can accept the situation that led to the failure; love that can forgive the repentant heart; and love that can treat a sinner as one who is good. It is the love that allowed God to measure that scoundrel Jacob, who had tricked his father, stolen his brother's birthright, and cheated his uncle, to measure him and find something left to love. It is the love that Jesus showed for the adulterous woman when he saved her from being stoned, and for Peter who had denied him. It is the love that measures each one of us, with all our failures and limitations, and still finds something of value to nurture, and encourage.

Prayer: *Thank you, God, for measuring us with eyes of love that see beyond who we are now to the persons we can become, with your help. May we look upon others in the same way, and measure them right, too. Amen.*

1. A Raisin in the Sun, *by Lorraine Hansberry. © 1959 by Lorraine Hansberry, (Published by Random House as a Signet Book, New American Library of World Literature, 1961).*

Embracing the Light

Seeing God in Jesus

No one has ever seen God; it is God the only Son, who is close to the Father's heart, who has made him known. (John 1:18)

God's love was revealed among us in this way: God sent his only Son into the world so that we might live through him. In this is love, not that we loved God but that he loved us. (1 John 4:9-10a)

One of the art projects I liked to use with children is a montage. First, we would choose a theme for our picture, and then we would look through magazines to find pictures to illustrate that theme. For example, if our theme was "water," we might select pictures of waterfalls and rivers, a water tower, raindrops, snow, a dishpan full of water, a bathtub or shower, water in a drinking glass, and water in a baptismal font. Each picture would show what water looks like, where it is found, what it does, or how it is used. After arranging the pictures attractively on a firm backing, we would glue them in place and entitle our montage "Water." Later we would use the picture in talking together about the use of water in the Sacrament of Baptism.

The Bible is like a montage. It has many different word pictures of God that help us "see" who God is and what God does. However, it is Jesus who has made God concrete and visible to us. All of our individual and communal pictures of God must be judged by the God we see in Jesus: a God who acts in love to teach us, heal us, worry over us, weep for us, judge us, forgive us, and offer us eternal life.

Prayer: *Thanks be to you, God, for your self-revealing love in Jesus. Amen.*

Moving Pictures

Such a very large crowd gathered around him that he got into a boat on the sea and sat there, while the whole crowd was beside the sea on the land. He began to teach them many things in parables. (Mark 4:1-2a)

The followers of Jesus remembered and recorded many of the word pictures he used to describe God. The most familiar, of course, is "Father." Jesus taught his disciples to pray, "Our Father, who art in heaven…" "Your Father knows what you need before you ask," he said. He urged the disciples to "be merciful, as your Father is merciful." Jesus pictured God as a loving, caring, forgiving father, suggesting it was possible to enjoy a close, personal relationship with God, based on love and trust, rather than fear.

Jesus pictured God in other ways, however. The parables his disciples remembered are full of metaphors drawn from every day life to describe God. For example:

God is the one who seeks out the lost, the Shepherd who searches for the lost lamb, the Woman who looks for her lost coin.

God is the one who rejoices when the lost return, and welcomes them with open arms, as the father welcomed the Prodigal Son.

God is the Sower planting seeds in the soil, the Host who invites friends to a marriage feast, the Good Neighbor who shows mercy to a stranger, a Rich Man who entrusts his wealth to his servants, an

Employer who is more than generous with his workers, a Mother Hen who gathers her chicks under her wings.

Note that Jesus' pictures of God are never static. They are more like videos than photos, more like movies than still pictures. God is always doing something in these pictures: seeking out the lost and rejoicing over their return, planting seeds, hosting a feast, showing kindness to a stranger, trusting workers and treating them fairly, protecting God's children. For Jesus, God is the One who acts in our everyday lives, the One who loves us unceasingly. This is good news indeed!

Prayer: *Living and loving God, who has never abandoned us, we thank you for all the ways you stay involved in our lives. May we be as faithful in our response to you. Amen.*

A Giving God

For great is [God's] steadfast love toward us, and the faithfulness of the Lord endures forever. Praise the Lord! (Psalm 117:2)

Jesus was many things: preacher, teacher, healer, miracle-worker, and friend. Since church education has been a focus of my ministry, Jesus' skill as a teacher has always interested me. He was a master at using stories from everyday life to teach his followers about the love of God. His parables, and others in the Bible, are still useful teaching tools. But if we look around, sometimes in surprising places, we can find other stories that help us discover new truths about God.

Shel Silverstein's picture book story about the Giving Tree who loved a little boy is one of my favorite modern-day parables.[1] When the boy is little, the Tree gladly provides branches for climbing, apples for eating, and shade from the sun. When the boy becomes a young adult in need of money, the Tree lets him take its apples to sell. When he marries and has a family, the Tree provides lumber for him to build a house. When he faces the crisis of middle age, the Tree lets him use its trunk for a boat so he can sail away from it all. The boy loves the Tree for all it has given him, and, in his old age, he comes back to it. The Tree is sad, for all it has left is its stump. It has nothing more to give. But the boy, who is now an old man, says, "That's all right. All I need is a place to sit and rest." Once again the Tree is happy. "Be my guest," it says, "be my guest."

Prayer: *God, you are like that Giving Tree. You provide for all our needs, at great cost to yourself, and we can always find a home in your love. Thank you. Amen.*

1. The Giving Tree, *by Shel Silverstein (HarperCollins, 1964).*

Embracing the Light

A Love That
Will Not Let Us Go

But while he was still far off, his father saw him and was filled with such compassion; he ran and put his arms around him and kissed him. Then the son said to him, "Father, I have sinned against heaven and before you; I am no longer worthy to be called your son." But the father said to his slaves…"Let us eat and celebrate; for this son of mine was dead and is alive again; he was lost and is found!"
(Luke 15:20-24, sel.)

When my oldest granddaughter Katie came home for Christmas her first year in college, she brought me her copy of Ron Hansen's novel, *Atticus*,[1] a book she had read and discussed in a freshman seminar. She knew I loved mysteries and the plot was full of unexpected twists and turns. As the story unfolded, it also became clear that the plot was inspired by Jesus' parable of the prodigal son. In fact, in the last chapter, one of the characters recalls a folktale she had heard in college "about a father's pursuit of a son who'd run far away, from one world to the next. The father called to him, 'Please come back!' But his son looked across the great gulf between them and shouted to him, 'I can't go that far!' So his father yelled to his son, 'Then just come back halfway!' But his boy replied, 'I can't go back halfway!' And finally his father shouted, 'Walk back as far as you can! I'll go the rest of the way!'"

A father's love for an errant child is the theme of Jean Louis Forain's etching, "The Return of the Prodigal,"[2] a reproduction of which has hung in our home for many years. Against the stark background of a distant farmstead, a young man, his hat and walking stick tossed hastily aside, kneels with bowed head before an older, bearded man who has rushed out to meet him on the road. The man is bending toward the youth, drawing him near, his hands firmly placed on his shoulders, as if to hold on to him forever.

One day I found our younger son, then about four years old, staring up at this picture. Stephen looked at me and asked, "Why won't he let that man go?" As I told him Jesus' story about a father's all-encompassing love for his wayward and repentant son, I hoped he would always remember the love God has for all of us, errant children though we are, a love that will never let us go.

Prayer: *O Love, that wilt not let me go,*
          I rest my weary soul in thee;
          I give thee back the life I owe,
          That in thine ocean depths its flow
          May richer, fuller be.[3]

1. Atticus, *by Ron Hansen. New York: HarperCollins, 1996.*

2. *Jean Louis Forain (1852-1931), a French Impressionist painter, lithographer, watercolorist, and etcher, was best known for his political cartoons and social satires. However, he also had great sympathy for the poor and the unfortunate, and his emotional power as an etcher was frequently compared to that of Rembrandt.*

3. *George Matheson, 1882. The entire hymn is included in the* Pilgrim Hymnal *(The Pilgrim Press, 1952).*

The Unseen Presence

And I will ask the Father, and he will give you another Advocate, to be with you forever. This is the Spirit of truth, whom the world cannot receive, because it neither sees him nor knows him. You know him, because he abides with you, and he will be in you.…The Advocate, the Holy Spirit, whom the Father will send in my name, will teach you everything, and remind you of all that I have said to you.
(John 14:16-17, 26)

Some years ago a small group of Russian peasants met for worship, knowing that their gathering was illegal and they could be arrested if detected. Suddenly the door of the room flew open. An agent of the secret police, followed by his men, entered. The officer commanded his men to take down the names of everyone present, and warned the worshippers that it would be dangerous for them not to report to answer the charges in court.

When the agent and his men turned to leave, an old man in the group stopped him, saying, "You have overlooked one name." The officer asked his men to count the people again. The number was the same. "You are wrong," he told the old man. "I have all your names."

"No," the old man insisted. "You have overlooked one."

"Who is it then?" the officer shouted. "Who is this unseen presence?"

"The Spirit of our risen Lord, Jesus Christ," the old man said firmly. "He is here with us."

The perplexed officer shook his head. "You Christians and your Holy Spirit," he said impatiently. "Well, bring him with you when you answer these charges!"

And, of course, they did!

Prayer: *Like the air we breathe but cannot see, like the love we feel from our family when we are away from home, like the courage that comes to us when we are in danger, your Holy Spirit is always with us, God, guiding and sustaining us, comforting and forgiving us, encouraging us and giving us strength. Thank you. Amen.*

CHRISTIAN YEAR

Embracing the Light

Traditions

You shall put these words of mine in your heart and soul, and you shall bind them as a sign on your hand, and fix them as an emblem on your forehead. Teach them to your children, talking about them when you are at home and when you are away, when you lie down and when you rise. Write them on the doorposts of your house and on your gates. (Deuteronomy 11:18-20a)

Each year when the holidays are over, I spend a day taking down my decorations and putting them away. This is always a time-consuming process for me, because each decoration brings back memories of past celebrations: Christmas as a child, as a young married woman delivering my first son just before Christmas, as the parent of a growing family, as a new widow, as a grandmother. I think of the family members and good friends who made or bought many of the decorations for us, and the people who introduced us to customs that soon became our own. I hold them all in my heart as I work.

It was not until after my older son was married that I realized how important our holiday traditions were to our children. Around Thanksgiving, Philip said casually, "Tell me, where can we get an Advent wreath to use this year? And we'll need a set of worship services too."

I hoped the expression on my face did not give away what I was thinking. *This is the son who grumbled about family worship times?*

Who fought his brother and sisters over whose turn it was to light and blow out the candles? Who giggled through the carol his younger sister was struggling to accompany on the piano? Who complained about having to sit through our Christmas morning worship before opening his presents? Things do change, I thought. Now a parent himself, Philip was genuinely concerned about passing on his heritage of faith to his then two-year-old son, and he was reaching back to the traditions of his own childhood to do so. He understood that traditions and rituals, in the home and at church, help a family develop a sense of identity, a common faith, and shared values.

I ordered an Advent wreath and candles for him that year, and sent him a set of worship liturgies to use each week. His wife Sue reported that they had faithfully observed Advent every Sunday, even though my grandson had played his kazoo all through one service. (Some things never change.) A new tradition was born!

Prayer: *God of the past, the present, and the future, give us the wisdom, time, and energy to pass on the traditions of our faith in ways that will help generations yet to come understand and celebrate the power and goodness of your love. Amen.*

Thoughts of Mary

Joseph also went from the town of Nazareth in Galilee to Judea, to the city of David called Bethlehem, because he was descended from the house and family of David. He went to be registered with Mary, to whom he was engaged and who was expecting a child. While they were there, the time came for her to deliver her child. And she gave birth to her firstborn son and wrapped him in bands of cloth, and laid him in a manger, because there was no place for them in the inn. (Luke 2:4-7)

The beautiful stories of Jesus' birth in the gospels of Luke and Matthew have always had great meaning for me, but never so much as the year when my husband and I were awaiting the birth of our first child. Perhaps because my name was also Mary, I felt a great kinship with that young mother who had delivered her child in a cave in Bethlehem. I could identify with Mary's weariness at the end of her long journey, the heaviness of her body, and the anxiety she must have felt about her impending labor. As I felt the new life stirring within me, waiting to be born, I could imagine the hopes and dreams Mary must have had for the baby she carried.

When our son was born on December 23, like Mary I knew the joy and wonder of being part of God's creative process. And when family and friends came to admire our son, I experienced the pride Mary must have felt when the shepherds and wise men came to see her first-born son. Life was rich and full indeed.

For Mary, as for me, there were more children and many years of family life with all its joys and challenges. But then, sometime after Jesus' twelfth birthday, Joseph died and Mary had to assume the difficult role of being a single parent to her maturing family. As another Mary who was widowed too soon, I know how Mary must have questioned her ability to meet all her responsibilities without the support of a loving husband.

I think about Mary each year at Christmas. My first-born son has long passed the age when Mary's son began his ministry. He is established in his career, happily married, and the father of two. Mary's son was an itinerant preacher, without a permanent job or home or family. No grandchildren for her, no daughter-in-law to enjoy, no home to visit. Only wonder at Jesus' miracles and teachings, pride in his courage, fear for his safety, and a determination to stand by him to the end. My heart goes out to Mary for the "normal" joys in life that she missed, but at the same time I marvel at her acceptance of her lot and her faithfulness to God's purpose and will. To me, the miracle of Christmas is not just that God has come to us in Christ, but also what God enables us to do in response to Christ's presence.

Prayer: *God, in this Christmas season, give us the faith of Mary.*
          Help us also trust in your purpose and will, as revealed by
          her son, our Lord and Savior, Jesus Christ. Amen.

If Only

In the beginning was the Word, and the Word was with God, and the Word was God....And the Word became flesh and lived among us, and we have seen his glory, the glory as of a father's only son, full of grace and truth. (John 1:1, 14)

Some years ago, in his syndicated religious news column, Louis Cassels told the story[1] of a man who begged off going to a Christmas Eve service with his family. He was a good man, a kind man, a man who treated others with justice and generosity. But he was also an honest man, and he would not pretend to celebrate what he did not believe. "I simply cannot understand why or how God could become one of us," he told his wife. "It just doesn't make any sense."

As the family went off to church without him, the man noticed that snow was beginning to fall. *We'll have a white Christmas*, he thought as he sat down to read beside the fire. The wind came up, and soon he heard thumping noises against the living room window. He went to the door to check, and found a flock of birds huddled in the storm. In their desperate search for shelter, they had tried to fly through his window. *I can't let them freeze*, the man said to himself. He put on his coat, went out to the barn where his children kept their horses, turned on a light, and opened the door wide. It was no use. The birds would not come in, not even when he scattered bread crumbs on the path to guide them, or waved his arms to shoo them in. *They are too afraid to trust me*, he said to himself. *If only I could be a bird myself for a few minutes, perhaps I could lead them to safety.*

Just then the church bells pealed the glad news of Christmas. The man stood thinking for a moment, then knelt down in the snow. "Now I understand why you had to do it," he whispered. "Now I believe."

Prayer: *You became one of us, God, not just for a few minutes, but for the span of a human life, that in the life, death, and resurrection of Jesus, we might come to trust in your love and believe in your way. God, we believe! Amen.*

1. *"The Parable of the Birds," in a newspaper column distributed through United Press International in 1969, and retold in many versions since in newspapers and radio broadcasts.*

What's on Your Christmas List?

[Jesus] himself said, "It is more blessed to give than to receive." (Acts 20:35, sel.)

God loves a cheerful giver. (2 Corinthians 9:7b)

What do you want for Christmas this year? How often children are asked that question as the holidays approach! Rarely does anyone inquire about the gifts they plan to give others. Busy parents find it hard to schedule time to shop with their children or help them with homemade gifts. They put all their energy into satisfying their children's wish lists, rather than letting them experience the joy of giving, which is such an important part of celebrating the birth of Jesus.

Two of my grandchildren grew up in the community where I made my home. Each December, when they were younger, I took them out individually for lunch and shopping so they could choose small Christmas gifts for their parents and one another. Their parents sent money and some suggestions, but the children made their own choices after visiting their favorite stores and looking over all the merchandise. After they made their purchases, I helped them wrap and tag their gifts. I can still remember five-year-old Kenny beaming with pride every time his father wore the Bugs Bunny tie he picked out at the post office, and his mother wore her rainbow earrings. His sister Katie, then ten, was so caught up in the spirit of giving that year that she used tickets earned at a spring carnival at church to buy gifts for her mother and grandmothers for Mother's Day. She was overjoyed at finding just the right thing for each of us. (My gift was a pen to hang around my neck!)

The joy of giving does not always come naturally to children, or adults, for that matter. On their first Christmas shopping excursions, my grandchildren were often distracted by things they saw and wanted for themselves. With practice, however, they gradually learned to focus on the needs of others instead of their own. They learned to be "cheerful givers," taking delight in surprising loved ones with gifts they had chosen with great thought and care.

The church depends on people who have discovered this spirit of joyful generosity, and embraced it as a way of life. When "cheerful giving" becomes a habit, there is no end to what we can accomplish as a community of faith.

Prayer: *Generous God, giver of all good things, help us find ways to practice "cheerful giving" so we too can learn that it is more blessed to give than receive. Amen.*

True Gifts

I was hungry and you gave me food, I was thirsty and you gave me something to drink, I was a stranger and you welcomed me, I was naked and you gave me clothing, I was sick and you took care of me, I was in prison and you visited me....As you did it to one of the least of these who are members of my family, you did it to me.
(Matthew 25:35-36, 40)

Birthdays and presents seem to go together, but on Christmas, the only one who doesn't get a gift is Jesus, the one whose birthday it is that we celebrate. A story by Leo Tolstoy[1] suggests how we can remedy that situation.

Tolstoy introduces us to Martin, a lonely old shoemaker, who lived and worked alone in a basement apartment. After many hours of reading his Bible and thinking about Jesus, Martin became convinced that Jesus would come to visit him the very next day. That morning, he rose early, made ready his home and food for his guest, and then sat down to work and wait. He had guests, all right, but Jesus never came. Instead he invited an old soldier in for tea, and gave a weary young mother and child food and clothing. He even helped settle a quarrel between a young boy and the old woman he tried to rob.

Martin had been so sure that Jesus would visit him that day, but when evening came without his knock on the door, Martin gave up hope that he would come. Disappointed, he picked up his Bible to read before going to bed. It fell open to a passage from the Gospel of Matthew, and he heard the voices of those he had helped asking in turn, "Didn't you recognize me, Martin?" Then he heard a new voice speak, a gentle, warm voice: "Martin, anything you did for my brothers and sisters here, however humble, you did for me."

Martin sighed. He understood now that he had entertained his heavenly guest after all, and he knew what kind of gifts were on Jesus' Christmas birthday list.

Prayer: *Come, Lord Jesus, be our guest. There is room in our hearts for you, and time in our lives to share your love and our possessions with those who are in need. Amen.*

1. *"Where Love Is, There God Is Also" from* What Men Live By and Where Love Is, There God Is Also, *by Leo Tolstoy. Fleming H. Revell Company. The story has been retold in a picture book version,* The Shoemaker's Dream, *with illustrations by Mashiro Kasuya and English text by Mildred Schell (Shiko Sha Company, Ltd., 1980; Judson Press, 1982).*

Embracing the Light

Walking in the Light

Again Jesus spoke to them, saying, "I am the light of the world. Whoever follows me will never walk in darkness but will have the light of life." (John 8:12)

One of the joys of Christmas for me is discovering a new story to share with my family during the holiday. As I was browsing in a book store one year, I found *The Christmas Candle*,[1] an original fable illustrated with beautiful oil paintings that told the story of Thomas, a young man on his way home to spend Christmas Eve with his family. Realizing that the candle in his lantern is about to go out, Thomas stops at a shop to buy another to light his way home. He scorns the fanciful, sculpted candles in the shop as a waste of time and money, and asks instead for one that is simple and inexpensive. The shopkeeper sells him a cheap candle, but cautions him that he might find it costly in the end.

Thomas sets out for home again, and along the way encounters needy persons who, in the light of the candle, look surprisingly like members of his own family. He gives his cloak to a frail beggar woman who looks like his mother. He offers his knapsack and its contents to an innkeeper in exchange for a room for a sick young man who resembles his brother. When he encounters a small child, he has to tell her he has nothing left to give. Arriving home empty-handed, he is greeted by his family, but in the candle's light his sister's face becomes the face of the child he had left behind in the street. He excuses himself to search her out and bring her home to share their Christmas feast.

The candle had truly "illuminated" the way for Thomas—not just the way home, but the Way of Christ.

Prayer: *God, we thank you for Jesus, who has brought the light of your love into our world and taught us to think of all those in need as our brothers and sisters, parents and children. May we be compassionate, healing, helping followers of the Way. Amen.*

1. The Christmas Candle, *by Richard Paul Evans, illustrated by Jacob Collins (New York: Simon & Schuster Books for Young Readers, 1998). All proceeds from this book are donated to a nonprofit organization founded by the author to build shelter-assessment facilities for abused children waiting to be placed in foster homes.*

The Word Made Flesh

And the Word became flesh and lived among us, and we have seen his glory, the glory as of a father's only son, full of grace and truth. (John 1:14)

According to some Christian traditions, the Wise Men did not reach the manger in Bethlehem until twelve days after the birth of Jesus. That is why many people observe the "twelve days of Christmas" and celebrate the Day of the Three Kings on January 6.

On a tropical island in the South Pacific, however, there is a church that observes Christmas all year long! During World War II, the American troops built an airstrip on the island. The chaplain and his crew tried to tell the native people about their Christian faith, but the islanders were slow to respond. By Christmas 1943, the servicemen had orders to move on. Before they left, they gave a big farewell Christmas party for the islanders, complete with makeshift presents, and tried to explain the meaning of Christmas.

A few years later, when the war was over, this same chaplain stopped at the island on his way to India, where he planned to serve as a missionary. The chaplain was greeted with great excitement and taken to see something special, a church the islanders had built. Over the doorway was a crude sign: "This is our church built on the faith and brotherly love which we know is." The chaplain stayed for the simple service. The songs were all Christmas carols, for these were the only ones the islanders knew.

"After you left," one explained, "we built the church to worship the God of Jesus. We worship him with the only service we know, the Christmas service. Every day is Christmas here. Every day the Christ Child is born anew. Our gift is love. We call our church the 'Christmas Church.'"

The Word of God became flesh in Jesus Christ, and that incarnation continues in us, the Body of Christ, when we live and act with love, compassion, and justice wherever we find ourselves. Let us never forget the privilege and responsibility we have of being the means by which others may come to know and accept the love of God.

Prayer: *God, keep our hearts sound, our lives pure, our thinking straight, and our spirits humble, that we may be true bearers of your Word to one another throughout your world. Amen.* (Adapted from a prayer by St. Augustine.)

The Cross on the Manger

Christ Jesus, who though he was in the form of God, did not regard equality with God as something to be exploited, but emptied himself, taking the form of a slave, being born in human likeness. And being found in human form, he humbled himself and became obedient to the point of death—even death on a cross. (Philippians 2:5b-8)

Some years ago the news media carried a story about a minister who decided to surprise his congregation by setting up an outdoor crèche. He had worked on the Nativity figures in his workshop all fall, and knew just where he would arrange them: on the corner of the church yard where the street light would shine down on them at night, just as the star of Bethlehem had shone on the manger long ago. The minister hummed Christmas carols to himself as he carefully set the Nativity figures in place. Then he waited impatiently for night to come. *How happy people will be when they see the crèche!* he thought. *When they see the baby in the manger, they will remember how much God loves them.*

The minister was unprepared for the angry phone calls that came from members of his congregation that night. "We can't have a Nativity scene like that!" they complained. "You're going to have to move it right away!" The minister was hurt and disappointed. *I worked so hard on those figures,* he said to himself. *I thought they were beautiful. Perhaps I was wrong.* He went outside to look at the crèche again. "Ah, now I understand," he sighed. "The street light has cast its shadow on the manger, and it looks like a cross. I hadn't counted on that."

A cross on the manger confuses us. It is a paradox we do not understand, an absurdity, a mystery. A cross means suffering, defeat, death, an end of life. A manger signifies joy, hope, birth, and a new beginning. A cross on a manger disturbs us, especially at Christmas. We want to be happy, to celebrate the love that led God to become one of us in that baby in the manger. We don't want to think about the man Love led to the cross. And yet, that cross, that empty cross, is the reason for our celebration. Jesus' birth would have been insignificant, had it not been for the man he became. His life, death, and resurrection are what give meaning to his birth.

Hymn writer Brian Wren put it this way:

> *Sing my song backwards, from end to beginning,*
> *Friday to Monday, from dying to birth.*
> *Nothing is altered, but hope changes everything.*
> *Sing Resurrection and peace upon earth!*[1]

Prayer: *God, may we never forget the true source of our joy at*
         Christmas. Amen.

---

1. *From* Faith Looking Forward: The Hymns & Songs of Brian Wren with many Tunes by Peter Cutts. © *1983, Hope Publishing Company*

You Did It For Me

Wise men from the East came to Jerusalem, asking, "Where is the child who has been born king of the Jews? For we observed his star at its rising, and have come to pay him homage." (Matthew 2:1-2)

Tradition has it there were three wise men, but Henry Van Dyke suggested in his touching story[1] that there might have been a fourth man named Artaban who made the trip.

Artaban, like the others, had sold all his possessions to buy precious jewels to lay before the newborn king. However, it took him much longer than twelve days to reach Bethlehem. On the way, he had stopped to help a sick man, and when he arrived in Bethlehem the Holy Family had already left.

For thirty-three years Artaban searched for his king, not among the mighty but among the poor, the lonely, and the oppressed. A rabbi had told him he would find his king among those who needed his love most. The king eluded him, but Artaban found many in need of his help. One by one, he used up his precious jewels. By the time he reached Jerusalem he had only one pearl left. It was Passover time, but the city had an air of gloomy excitement. Artaban was horrified to learn that the king he sought was to be crucified the next day. Thinking that his last pearl might buy the king's freedom, he went to offer it, only to be side-tracked again by the cries of a young girl who was about to be sold as a slave. He could not ignore her cries for help, and offered his last gift for the king as ransom.

Suddenly there was a great earthquake, and stones came tumbling down from a nearby building, knocking the aged Artaban to the ground. As he lay dying, he was heard to ask in a weak voice, "But when did I see you, Lord? I have looked for you all these years, and never brought you my gifts or served you." And another voice was heard, "anything you did for one of my brothers here, however humble, you did for me."

Prayer: *God, we thank you for all those who walk in the footsteps of Jesus and follow his way of love, for it is through them that we come to know you and trust in your goodness. Make us ever willing to be side-tracked from our personal goals whenever and wherever persons in need call out for our love. Amen.*

---

1. The Story of the Other Wise Man, *by Henry Van Dyke (Harper & Brothers, 1895, 1923). The story has been retold by Pamela Kennedy and illustrated by Robert Barrett as* The Other Wise Man *(Ideals Children's Books, 1989).*

Anno Domini:
The Year of Our Lord

For everything there is a season, and a time for every matter under heaven. (Ecclesiastes 3:1)

Church bulletins used to be dated "Anno Domini," meaning "in the year of our Lord," but the abbreviation "AD" is not used much any more. Most of us now divide the time before and after the birth of Christ into "BCE" (Before the Christian Era) and "CE" (Christian Era). "AD" had merit, however. It reminded us that all of time belongs to God, and that we live in an age divided from all other ages by the moment when God became one of us in Jesus Christ. It reminded us that, year after year, Christians through the ages have remembered and celebrated the stories of this marvelous event that ushered in a new era in history. For us, each new year is "Anno Domini, the year of our Lord." This "Liturgical" or "Church Year" begins with Advent, and continues through Christmas, Epiphany, Lent, Holy Week, Easter, and Pentecost.

The season of Lent is a serious time. In these forty days leading up to Holy Week and Easter, we remember that Jesus began his ministry with a forty-day retreat from the world. Off in the wilderness by himself, he prayed and thought about what God wanted him to do with his life. He resisted the temptation to put the power he had received from God to his own use. And he went back into the world, strengthened and ready to carry out his mission.

During Lent, we too retreat from the world to spend extra time praying and thinking about what God expects from us. We too face up to the things that tempt us, and ask God's help in standing firm against them. And if we have faltered and fallen, we ask God's forgiveness and mercy. In this way, we prepare to hear the good news of Christ's resurrection and receive strength and encouragement to live a new life with God.

Prayer: *In this busy world, God, where our time seems to belong to everyone but us, you call us to slow down, retreat from our everyday routines, and reclaim the time you have given us to meditate and pray about your purpose for our lives. Help us to hear your call, and respond, that we might be ready for the miracle of Easter. Amen.*

Priorities

Jesus, full of the Holy Spirit, returned from the Jordan and was led by the Spirit in the wilderness, where for forty days he was tempted by the devil. (Luke 4:1-2a)

After his baptism, Jesus knew he had to get his priorities straight. He understood his mission was to make visible God's love for his people, and encourage them to love God in return. But how was he going to do this? He needed to go off by himself to have time to think. He left the Jordan River valley and went into the barren mountain wilderness to be alone.

For forty days, Jesus struggled with the temptation to take the easy way out. He knew very well what the people expected and wanted: a king who would provide for all of their needs, a military leader who would help them overthrow their Roman conquerors, a miracle worker who would make everything right in their world. *If I used the power I have from God to give the people what they want, they will surely follow me,* he thought, *but for all the wrong reasons.* Jesus realized that people who were impressed with handouts or force or magic would miss the point of his coming. They would not understand that the only real power in the world is the love that comes from God. *My life must be an expression of that love,* Jesus said to himself. *That must be my priority.*

The forty days of Lent offer a time for us to reflect on our lives and put our priorities in order. It is a time for considering the "easy ways" that tempt us: trying to make it rich in video lottery or the gambling halls, cheating on our tax returns, driving over the speed limit, overcharging our customers, putting in inflated timesheets, being unfaithful to a spouse, foregoing our child's activity to watch our favorite television show, excusing ourselves by saying "Everyone's doing it." Lent is a time to follow Jesus' example, a time to listen to God's call, a time to decide to follow the way of love.

Prayer: *God, help us take time to get our priorities straight. Help us turn aside from the easy ways of the world to follow your way, the way of self-giving love. Amen.*

Keeping Lent

A scribe then approached and said, "Teacher, I will follow you wherever you go." And Jesus said to him, "Foxes have holes, and birds of the air have nests; but the Son of Man has nowhere to lay his head." (Matthew 8:19-20)

Jesus gave up a normal family life with a wife and children, the security of a home, a job that paid a decent wage, the approval of his hometown neighbors, the chance for political power, a pain-free existence, and finally even life itself, all precious things to most human beings. He gave them up in order to give his life to God on our behalf.

Every year we are asked, "What are you giving up for Lent this year?" Too often, we "sacrifice" the sweets we should quit eating in order to lose weight, or things we wouldn't dream of doing anyway. Talking about what we're going to "give up" puts the emphasis in the wrong place: on us, and our needs. The true meaning of "sacrifice" is giving up something of value for the sake of another. The emphasis is on others, not ourselves. Lent is a time for real sacrifices, not pretend. We should be asking one another, "What are you giving up for God's sake during Lent? What are you giving up for the sake of your family? What are you giving up for the sake of your neighbors, far and near?"

An author, whose name is unknown, put it this way:

> Let us keep Lent.
> Let us not kneel and pray,
> forego some trifle every day,
> fast—and then take sacrament—
> and then
> lend tongue to slander, hold ancient grudge,
> deny
> the very Lord whom we would glorify.
>
> Let us keep Lent.
> Let our hearts grow in grace,
> let God's light shine till each illumined face
> will be a testament,
> read by everyone,
> that hate is buried; self, crucified; newborn
> the spirit that shall rise on Easter morn.
> Let us keep Lent.

Prayer: *Let us keep Lent, God, in this way. Amen.*

Repent, and Believe

Jesus came to Galilee, proclaiming the good news of God, and saying, "The time is fulfilled, and the kingdom of God has come near; repent, and believe in the good news." (Mark 1:14-15)

"Repent, and believe in the good news!" Most Christians see repentance as a prerequisite for receiving God's love and forgiveness. We don't eat unless we are hungry. We don't see a doctor unless we are sick. We don't fix the roof until it leaks. And we don't ask God to forgive us until we admit that we have done wrong and are sorry for our actions. Then, wonder of wonders, we discover God's love and forgiveness have been there waiting for us all along, just as Jesus had promised, and we are made new.

John Newton was an English slave trader who repented of his unjust ways and became a beloved Anglican pastor and hymn-writer. He described his experience of repentance, forgiveness, and new life this way:

> *Amazing grace! How sweet the sound*
> *that saved a wretch like me!*
> *I once was lost, but now am found,*
> *was blind but now I see.*
>
> *The Lord has promised good to me,*
> *his word my hope secures;*
> *he will my shield and portion be*
> *as long as life endures.*[1]

Lent is a time for repentance and renewal. It is a time for taking a serious look at our lives, and admitting that we fail to measure up to the standards God has given us in Jesus. It is a time for confessing our sins and asking God's forgiveness. It is a time for receiving God's love and mercy. It is a time for beginning a new life of Love.

Prayer: *The time is fulfilled, God, and your reign is here. We confess we have fallen short of your plan for us, and we are sorry. Forgive us, and help us to believe in your way of love. Amen.*

1. *From a hymn by John Newton, 1779.*

Spring Cleaning

Have mercy on me, O God, according to your steadfast love; according to your abundant mercy blot out my transgressions. Wash me thoroughly from my iniquity, and cleanse me from my sin....Create in me a clean heart, O God, and put a new and right spirit within me.
(Psalm 51:1-2, 10)

When I was growing up in Gaylord, Minnesota, my mother and most of the other women in that small town observed the ritual of thoroughly cleaning their homes in the fall and the spring. It is a habit I have never been able to break. In the fall I get my home ready for winter, washing windows, cleaning cupboards and drawers, washing and airing bedding, getting out warmer blankets and quilts, putting away summer clothes and getting out winter things. In the spring the process is reversed. I clean the house thoroughly, take winter coats to the cleaners, collect clothing and household items for the spring rummage sale at church, get rid of all the rubbish that has collected in the garage, take the stacks of newspapers to the recycling center, and open the windows to let in the fresh air of spring.

It has always seemed appropriate to me that the season of Lent coincides with my annual spring cleaning urge. These forty days afford us time to sort through our lives and throw out the trash: our selfish demands to have our own way, the grudges we hold against those who have hurt us, our tendency to gossip about our friends, our reluctance to share our time and resources with others, our indifference to the plight of the poor. The list goes on and on. Lent is a time to ask God to forgive us for our failures, and help us start over in clean, orderly, loving ways.

Prayer: *Love, light a candle in my heart that I may see inside*
the fearful web of selfishness, of arrogance and pride,
that traps my spirit, snares my will, entangles me in sin.
Love, light a candle in my heart that I may see within.

Love, light a candle in my heart that I may see inside
to sweep away this tangled web that I have tried to hide.
Redeem my spirit, free my will, and help me to begin.
Love, light a candle in my heart that I may see within.

Love, light a candle in my heart that I may see inside
and find compassion, joyful hope, and faith all now abide
within the place where once a web of selfishness had been.
Love, light a candle in my heart that I may see within.[1]

---

1. *Hymn text inspired by the prayer of an anonymous African girl in* Eerdman's Book of Famous Prayers: A Treasury of Christian Prayers through the Centuries, *compiled by Veronica Zundel (Lion Publishing/Wm. B. Eerdmans Publishing Company, 1984). The hymn is included in* Faith That Lets Us Sing, *words by Mary Nelson Keithahn, music by John D. Horman, Wayne Leupold Editions, Inc., 2016. Used by permission.*

Embracing the Light

Making Things Right

Zacchaeus stood there and said to the Lord, "Look, half of my possessions, Lord, I will give to the poor; and if I have defrauded anyone of anything, I will pay back four times as much." Then Jesus said to him, "Today salvation has come to this house." (Luke 19:8-9)

The story of the short, little man from Jericho is a familiar one. Jesus was passing through Jericho on his way to Jerusalem for the Passover, and noticed Zacchaeus sitting in a tall sycamore tree. He had climbed the tree in order to get a good look at the rabbi everyone was talking about. Zacchaeus himself was not popular. He collected taxes for the Romans, and cheated his fellow Jews on a regular basis. They hated him for that, and would have nothing to do with him.

Jesus must have sensed his loneliness and guilt. He called Zacchaeus down from the tree and invited himself to dinner at his house! You can imagine what a shock this was to the neighbors! A faithful Jew would never eat with such a sinner.

Zacchaeus was, of course, changed by this experience. He was sincerely sorry for all the wrongs he had done, but he did not stop with words of repentance. He gave half of all his wealth to the poor, and returned four times what he had stolen.

The season of Lent is a time for repentance, for turning away from the wrongs we have done and turning back to God. But the story of

Zacchaeus reminds us that true repentance always leads to action, to sharing what we have with those who have less, and making things right for those we have hurt.

Prayer: *How sorry we are, God, for the problems we allow to exist in our world through our neglect and selfish ways. Help us make things right by sharing your gifts of time, talents and skills, and material means with those who are in need. Amen.*

Hosanna!

Then they brought the colt to Jesus and threw their cloaks on it; and he sat on it. Many people spread their cloaks on the road, and others spread leafy branches that they had cut in the fields. Then those who went ahead and those who followed were shouting, "Hosanna! Blessed is the one who comes in the name of the Lord! Blessed is the coming kingdom of our ancestor David! Hosanna in the highest heaven!" (Mark 11:7-10)

Jesus' triumphal entry into Jerusalem on what we now call Palm Sunday has been the subject of paintings by many artists through the years. Often the artists have included children in the crowds that greeted Jesus. They show the children waving palm branches, tossing flowers in his path, and singing "Hosanna!"

Hymn writers too have mentioned children in their Palm Sunday texts:

> *All glory, laud, and honor to thee, Redeemer, King,*
> *to whom the lips of children made sweet hosannas ring![1]*

> *"Hosanna, loud hosanna," the little children sang;*
> *through pillared court and temple, the lovely anthem rang;*
> *to Jesus, who had blessed them close folded to his breast,*
> *the children sang their praises, the simplest and the best.[2]*

And in many congregations today, it is always the children who process into worship waving palm branches on Palm Sunday.

Yet not one of the four Gospels mentions children in their accounts of this incident! Why do we always assume children were there to greet Jesus?

Perhaps it's because we know children love a parade and would have come along with their parents to watch Jesus enter the city. After all, it was a holiday time when families from all over were in Jerusalem for Passover. But perhaps it was also because of what Jeanette Threlfall hinted at in her hymn. We know Jesus loved and welcomed the children who came to see him, and they loved him in return. They trusted and believed what Jesus told them about God. They would have been the first to shout "Hosanna!" when Jesus came riding into Jerusalem that day.

Prayer: *God, let us always remember how Jesus valued and loved the children, and follow his example, not just on Palm Sunday but throughout the whole year. Amen.*

1. *Theodulph of Orleans, ninth century; translated by John Mason Neale, 1854. The entire hymn is in* The Pilgrim Hymnal *(The Pilgrim Press, 1958).*

2. *Jeanette Threlfall, 1873. The entire hymn is in* The New Century Hymnal *(The Pilgrim Press, 1995).*

Embracing the Light

Two Women Named Elizabeth

*And during supper Jesus…got up from the table, took off his outer robe,
and tied a towel around himself. Then he poured water into a basin
and began to wash the disciples' feet.…After he had washed their feet…
and had returned to the table, he said to them…"You call me Teacher
and Lord—and you are right, for that is what I am. So if I, your
Lord and Teacher, have washed your feet, you also ought to wash one
another's feet. For I have set you an example, that you also should do as
I have done to you."* (John 13:2-15, sel.)

When the first Queen Elizabeth ruled England, it was the custom
for Christian rulers to wash the feet of twelve poor men on Maundy
Thursday, as a sign of their Christ-like humility and desire to serve
the people. Queen Elizabeth observed the traditional ceremony, but
only after her servants had first carefully scrubbed and perfumed
the poor men's feet so that the queen would not be contaminated
or offended.

Two hundred years later, another English woman, Elizabeth Fry,
was playing with the youngest of her eight children when a friend
stopped by to tell her about the horrible conditions in a London
prison. Female prisoners did not have proper food, clothing, or
medical care. They spent their days gambling, drinking, and
fighting because there was nothing else to do. Often their babies
and young children were incarcerated with them. Elizabeth Fry
was so moved by this report that she determined to investigate
the women's plight herself. She began visiting the prison, despite

warnings that she would be robbed and harmed by the inmates. She persuaded officials to provide clean bedding for them, solicited donations of clothing and blankets from people she knew, started a school for the children, and held classes in sewing and reading for the women. She also helped the prisoners make simple rules for the group and elect leaders who could see that the rules were followed. Her love and concern for the women gave them hope, and because of her example, conditions in other prisons were improved too.

Two Elizabeths, but only one grasped the real reason for Jesus' symbolic action in washing his disciples' feet. Only one understood the challenge of his words, "Do as I have done to you."

Prayer: *Forgive us, God, when we substitute superficial, token actions for real service to the poor. Let us never rest until all your children enjoy the blessings that have come to us. Amen.*

Can Anything Good
Come Out of Suffering?

And they clothed him in a purple cloak; and after twisting some thorns into a crown, they put it on him. And they began saluting him, "Hail, King of the Jews!" They struck his head with a reed, spat upon him, and knelt down in homage to him. After mocking him, they stripped him of the purple cloak and put his own clothes on him. Then they led him out to crucify him. (Mark 15:17-20)

All of us have experienced suffering. We have watched beloved family members become ill or grow old and die. We have seen young life cut short by accidents or war. We have had to face our own loneliness and hurt, and eventually, our own mortality. Suffering is an unfortunate part of human existence. How can anything good come out of it?

Good Friday answers that question. Every year it reminds us that God has not wound us up like little toys and abandoned us to fend for ourselves until we wind down and fall over dead. God is with us throughout life, hurting when we hurt, weeping when we weep. God understands our suffering. After all, in Jesus Christ God willingly endured all the suffering that human beings can inflict upon one another. Yet even in that awful experience, Jesus was able to show love and concern for his mother and close friends who had followed him to the end. When he looked down at them from the cross and saw the pain and sorrow in their faces, Jesus asked them to care for one another as members of one family. In his suffering, he recognized the suffering of others, and compassion overcame self-pity.

My daughter-in-law Sue was diagnosed with breast cancer at the age of 47, and had a bilateral mastectomy a month later. Although her prognosis was excellent, this was a time of physical and emotional pain for her. Yet she wrote, "I've learned so much from this experience." She went on to tell of visiting a friend whose husband was in critical condition after a burst aneurysm. "We were able to talk about faith and death," she said. "This is a discussion I couldn't have had six months ago, and I think I really helped my friend."

Good Friday reminds us that suffering need not result in self-pity; rather, it can produce compassion and understanding for others who are in pain. Something good *can* come out of suffering!

Prayer: *God, we know that pain and loss are inevitable in our lives.
We pray that we will not wallow in self-pity at these
times, but use our suffering as a means of understanding
the suffering of others, so that we might comfort and care for
them as friends. Amen.*

Good Friday?

It was nine o'clock in the morning when they crucified him...When it was noon, darkness came over the whole land until three in the afternoon. At three o'clock Jesus cried out with a loud voice..."My God, my God, why have you forsaken me?"...Then Jesus gave a loud cry and breathed his last. (Mark 15:25, 33-34, 37)

Years ago one of my favorite television programs was called *You Are There*. The program dramatized different episodes from history in a way that made me feel as if I actually were there taking part in the events. I've often wished some kind of time travel were possible. I would like to go back to the time of Jesus and join those who followed him. I would like to see and hear for myself the wonderful things Jesus did and said. I would like to share in the events of the week we call "Holy": the entry into Jerusalem on Palm Sunday, the fellowship around the table on Maundy Thursday, the sorrow at the cross on Good Friday, and the joy of the empty tomb on Easter morning. I can only imagine how I would have felt on each of these occasions. One thing I do know, however: If I had been on that hill outside of Jerusalem, I doubt if I would have called that Friday "good." How can there be anything good in human suffering?

When our family visited in Japan in 1972, we heard about a woman who had found an answer to that question. Her name was Haruko Hoshino. Life had not been easy for her. Her husband was killed in China in World War II, leaving her with three small children to raise alone. Her oldest son, born disabled, died before he was twenty. In the years she cared for him, she visited many hospitals and religious sects, trying in vain to find a cure for his illness. It was not until she turned to the Christian church that she was able to receive comfort and strength from God, and see her suffering in a new light. Hearing about Christ's suffering on the cross, she realized God knew how she felt and shared her pain. She saw that God could use her suffering as a way to reach out to others with overwhelming problems. Haruko started to visit people in hospitals and in her neighborhood to tell them of God's love. She invited people into her home to sing and pray together and listen to her pastor share God's word. She sought to express God's love in her work as an artist. With God's help, she turned her suffering into something good. With God's help, we can do that too.

Prayer: *God, we know you feel our pain and walk with us when we suffer our "Fridays." Help us use what we have learned from our suffering to help others in pain. Make us channels of your compassion and kindness, that they too may know your love and mercy, and see that "Fridays" can be "good." Amen.*

You Will Be With Me

One of the criminals who were hanged there kept deriding him and saying, "Are you not the Messiah? Save yourself and us!" But the other rebuked him, saying, "Do you not fear God, since you are under the same condemnation? And we indeed have been condemned justly, for we are getting what we deserve for our deeds, but this man has done nothing wrong." Then he said, "Jesus, remember me when you come into your kingdom." He replied, "Truly I tell you, today you will be with me in Paradise." (Luke 23:39-43)

Much of what we suffer as humans is the result of wrong choices we have made. We decide to drink and drive, and someone is killed in a car crash. We eat too much and exercise too little, and have to deal with heart disease and diabetes. We party instead of studying and fail to get into the college of our choice. The list goes on and on.

When we finally have to suffer the consequences of our irresponsible and wrong choices, we are often overwhelmed by guilt. Like the second thief crucified beside Jesus, we feel we are only getting what we deserve. Yet if Jesus could pray for those who crucified him, "Father, forgive them for they know not what they do," perhaps we can believe God can forgive us too. Though we must accept responsibility for our actions, perhaps we can still believe Jesus' promise, "Truly I tell you, today you will be with me in Paradise."

I have always thought of the church as a fellowship of forgiven sinners. We have all fallen short of being the kind of persons God intends us to be. We all have deeds to repent, and consequences to face. Yet from Jesus' words on the cross, we know we are forgiven. And because we are forgiven sinners, we need to set aside our judgmental attitudes and open our arms to all who come in search of God's love.

Prayer: *God, we give thanks for Good Friday, because of the good things we have learned from it about your compasionate love, your promise of forgiveness and an eternal home, and your gift of a loving community to sustain us in our life here. Amen.*

I Know Their Sufferings

*Then the Lord said, "I have observed the misery of my people who
are in Egypt; I have heard their cry on account of their taskmasters.
Indeed I know their sufferings, and I have come down to deliver them."*
(Exodus 3:7-8a)

In an old Jewish legend, two villagers are talking together. The
first asks, "Friend, do you love me?" The other responds, "I love
you deeply." Then the first villager asks, "Do you know, my friend,
what gives me pain?" The second villager scoffs, "How can I know
what gives you pain?" The first replies, "If you do not know what
gives me pain, how can you say that you truly love me?"

When my husband died suddenly early on a Sunday morning,
family and friends came to be with me. But there was no one among
them who had lost a spouse, no one who had experienced the pain
I was feeling. Then a stranger appeared. Seeing the bewildered
look on my face, she explained, "You don't know me, but I took
care of your husband in the hospital. I heard about his death at
Mass this morning. I lost my first husband at an even younger
age. I just came to tell you that I know how you feel, and you will
survive." She was only there for a moment, but I will never forget
the compassion she showed to me in my sorrow. She was like an
angel bringing me a message from God, the same God who told
the Hebrew people, "I know your sufferings, and I have come to
deliver you."

God's willingness to feel our pain was made even more clear to us in Jesus, who endured the worst of life's experiences and knew what it was like to feel abandoned and alone. Because of Jesus, we know God understands our sorrow. We are not alone in our grief. God is right there with us, sharing our pain and caring for us through compassionate people like the nurse who came to see me on that Sunday morning after Mass.

Prayer: *How grateful we are, God, for your compassion and care for us in times of deepest sorrow and grief! Help us to be your angels of mercy to others in their suffering. Amen.*

Out of Death, Life

Whoever wishes to be great among you must be your servant, and whoever wishes to be first among you must be your slave; just as the Son of Man came not to be served but to serve, and to give his life a ransom for many. (Matthew 20:26-28)

Back in the black and white days of television, I used to enjoy a series called *Wagon Train* that dramatized the adventures of settlers heading West. In one episode, the wagon train was nearing the end of a long journey to California, when it was threatened by a band of outlaws demanding tribute from anyone crossing the desert. In his negotiations with the outlaws, the wagon master discovered that they were Mexican immigrants who had settled in California and lived peacefully there until gold was discovered. Then, despite having valid deeds to the land, they had been driven out by the people who flocked to California in search of gold. Homeless and bitter, they had turned to terrorizing the wagon trains carrying more California-bound settlers. An old man, one of the original immigrants, was their leader, assisted by a young man, born in the desert, who had known no other life.

One of the men on the wagon train was going to California to be a federal judge. He told the outlaws that their claim to the land was valid, and promised he would see that their lands were restored if they would let the wagon train pass unharmed. Those responsible for crimes against the wagon trains would, of course, still have to stand trial and face punishment.

The old leader loved his people. He knew their outlaw life was wrong, and he remembered what California had been like in the old days. He decided to trust the judge and guaranteed the wagon train safe passage. The younger leader, who knew no other life than that of an outlaw, was angry. Calling the old man a coward, he drew his gun to signal his men to attack the wagon train. The old man, in a desperate move to save his people, stepped in front of the gun and received the bullets himself. As he lay dying, he told the judge that he alone was responsible for the plundering and killing, because he had given the orders. He made the judge promise that with his death, the debt would be paid, and his people would be free to find a new life in California.

That television program took me back two thousand years to another time when a man willingly accepted the punishment his people deserved in order to give them a chance for a new life. His name was Jesus, and he died on a cross, but out of his death came life, for himself and for all humankind.

Prayer: *God, we give you thanks for Jesus, who took upon himself all the wrongs we have done and endured the suffering that should have been ours, thus assuring us of your forgiveness and love. Amen.*

He Died for Me

Then they all shouted out together, "Away with this fellow! Release Barabbas for us!" (This was a man who had been put in prison for an insurrection that had taken place in the city, and for murder.) Pilate, wanting to release Jesus, addressed them again; but they kept shouting, "Crucify, crucify him!"…He released the man they asked for…and he handed Jesus over as they wished. (Luke 23:18-21, 25)

The name of Barabbas vanishes from the scripture after his release, but Pär Lagerkvist has suggested what might have happened to him in his novel, *Barabbas*.[1] Lagerkvist's story begins as Barabbas is released from prison and tries unsuccessfully to return to his old ways, filling his nights with wine and women and his days with the adventures of his robber band. The troubled man cannot escape the Galilean and his followers. He witnesses the crucifixion, is there in the Garden on Easter morning, and seeks out Peter to ask him about Jesus.

Barabbas looks for rational explanations of his experiences. Prison darkness had dimmed his eyesight. That is why the Galilean seemed surrounded by an aura of light, why the sky seemed to grow dark when he died. His followers had stolen his body during the night. That is why the grave was empty on the third day. One thing could not be explained away, however. This Jesus of Nazareth had died in his place, and he was free to live the life he owed to Jesus. *Why*, Barabbas asked himself. *I didn't ask him to die for me. If Jesus were the Son of God, as his disciples said, why didn't he save himself? Did he want to suffer and die? Why would anyone want to do that? The Galilean used his power by not using it. He allowed others to decide his fate without interfering, and yet he got his own way. He was crucified instead of me. Why? Why?* Barabbas was a man of violence. He could not understand a man who sacrificed himself rather than hurt another. Jesus had died for him, and he could never be the same.

Barabbas turned to the followers of Jesus, wanting to believe, wanting to be forgiven, wanting to be accepted into their midst. But Barabbas was ugly, disfigured by a scar. He was a sinner to be feared. He was a doubter, asking disturbing questions. And he was the acquitted one, released in place of Jesus. The Christian community could never accept him for who he was, nor could they love him or forgive him. Perhaps that is why they could never help him to believe. Barabbas went through life without a faith, and the community that would not love or accept him lost someone who could have been their most powerful witness.

Prayer: *God, we are all Barabbas, failing to love you as we ought,
failing to understand your ways, failing to accept
your forgiveness. We are also those early Christians
who rejected him, turning away from sinners,
becoming impatient with doubters, finding ourselves
unable to forgive someone who has let us down or hurt us.
Forgive us, and help us to remember that we are all the
acquitted ones who live because Jesus died in our place.
Help us to love one another as he loved us. Amen.*

1. Barabbas, *by Pär Lagerkvist (1950) Vintage. 1st Vintage International Edition, 1989. Lagerkvist was awarded the Nobel Prize for Literature in 1951 for this novel.*

To My Children, I Leave...

Blessed be the God and Father of our Lord Jesus Christ! By his great mercy he has given us a new birth into a living hope through the resurrection of Jesus Christ from the dead, and into an inheritance that is imperishable, undefiled, and unfading, kept in heaven for you, who are being protected by the power of God through faith for a salvation ready to be revealed in the last time. (1 Peter 1:3-5)

After living in the same house for over twenty years, I moved into a new townhome in another city. Getting rid of the clutter was time-consuming but easy. I filled up eight huge city dumpsters with things I should have thrown away years ago. I had several garage sales, loaded up a van for the church rummage sale, sold some furniture and gave away other pieces, and took items to the local museum. However, I found I could not part with things I had inherited from my parents: a place setting of my grandmother's wedding dishes, antique silver pieces my mother used for holiday dinners, oil paintings done by the Swedish-American grandfather I never knew, a Victorian loveseat and rocker that graced the parlor of an elderly relative I remembered from childhood, the nineteenth-century walnut chest of drawers my great-grandmother had brought from Illinois to Iowa in an oxcart, my mother-in-law's little cherry rocker, my mother's desk and chair.

These things I inherited from my family keep me connected with them in a special way, and I hope to pass them on to my children and grandchildren some day. They are not my real inheritance, however. My real legacy from my parents is more intangible: honesty and integrity, a love of books and learning, an appreciation for music and the arts, compassion for people who are hurting, a desire for justice, a concern for children and an interest in their education, a willingness to work and give and serve, and a need to be part of the church and its ministries. These are things I hope my children and grandchildren will inherit from me. They are more important than any material things I can leave them.

Jesus died without any material possessions to pass on, but he left his disciples an inheritance nevertheless, something they passed on to their children and grandchildren and all of us who came after them. Jesus' legacy was a promise: *"Remember, I am with you always, to the end of the age."* (Matthew 28:20b) When God raised Jesus from the dead, God validated that promise. As a result, we don't ever have to be afraid again. No matter what happens to us in this life, God will be with us, and when we die God will continue to care for us. All we have to do is believe and trust in that promise. This is the inheritance that we celebrate on Easter, and every Sunday throughout the year.

Prayer: *Make us grateful heirs of your promise, God, and faithful in passing that promise on to others. May our words and deeds always assure them of your loving presence in their lives. Amen.*

Embracing the Light

A Name for Ourselves

*Then they said, "Come, let us build ourselves a city, and a tower with
its top in the heavens, and let us make a name for ourselves; otherwise
we shall be scattered abroad upon the face of the whole earth."*
(Genesis 11:4)

*When the day of Pentecost had come, they were all together in one
place....All of them were filled with the Holy Spirit and began to speak
in other languages, as the Spirit gave them ability....And at this sound
the crowd gathered and was bewildered, because each one heard them
speaking in the native language of each.* (Acts 2:1, 4, 6)

After eighteen years of MAD (Music, Art, and Drama) camp
and twelve original musical dramas, my composer colleague John
Horman and I believe in the power of the Holy Spirit, not just
at Pentecost but throughout the year! How else could we have
written and produced, year after year, a memorized, costumed,
choreographed musical with a broadly-graded group of unknown
talents by the end of a week at a residential church camp?

Although we usually focused on a single character from the Bible
or church history in our musicals, one year we wrote a "musical
review" that traced the work of the Holy Spirit from Creation
through the Day of Pentecost, as recorded in the Hebrew scriptures
and New Testament. There were songs for Adam and Eve, Cain
and Abel, Noah and sons, the citizens of Babel, Moses, Gideon,
Samson, Deborah, David, Delilah, Bathsheba, Jezebel, Elijah,

Jeremiah, Ezekiel, John the Baptist, Jesus, and the disciples! The whole point of the musical was that the stories of these biblical figures are our stories too. We are all created by the Spirit but try to take credit for who we are. We are gifted by the Spirit with talents and abilities, but often use these gifts "to make a name for ourselves," and are separated from one another by our selfishness. Prophets today, inspired by the Spirit, warn us that we are misusing our gifts, but we turn deaf ears to their words. We find it difficult to follow the way of Jesus who was blessed and led by the Spirit. Like the disciples, our only hope is that the Spirit will enter into each one of us, forgiving us and enabling us to share our gifts that they might bear fruit in the lives of others. We each need our own Pentecost experience to counteract our Babel tendencies.

Prayer: *Let your Holy Spirit enter into hearts on wings of dove.*
Let your will be at the center of our lives afire with love.
Find us, and fill us, O God.

Make us one with Christ in caring for the outcast and the lost,
that in joyful, selfless sharing we may never count the cost.
Find us, and form us, O God.[1]

---

1. © 1998, Abingdon Press. Used by permission. All rights reserved. These are the last two stanzas of "When the World Is Babbling 'Round Us" ("Prayer for Pentecost"), a hymn text reflecting on the Babel–Pentecost connection. It is included in Come Away With Me: A Collection of Original Hymns by Mary Nelson Keithahn and John D. Horman (Abingdon Press, 1998).

Embracing the Light

A Cheerful Giver: St. Nicholas

Remembering the words of the Lord Jesus…"It is more blessed to give than to receive." (Acts 20:35b)

In the fourth century, a young man named Nicholas was made bishop of Myra, a city in Lycia, a mountainous region along the southern coast of what is now Turkey. Many tales have been told about miracles he performed, but we remember him most for his generous, loving spirit.

Parents arranged the marriages of their children at this time, and a father had to provide a dowry for each daughter. A farmer might offer a plow and some seed to a prospective husband, a fisherman a boat and nets, and a shopkeeper a share in his business. It took a generous dowry to interest a rich husband. When Nicholas heard of a poor man who had three daughters, he knew he would not be able to provide dowries for them or care for them any longer. He would have to sell them as slaves.

Nicholas wanted to help the poor man and his daughters. He took all the gold he had and divided it into three sacks. When it was night, he quietly crept to the poor man's home, threw the three bags of gold into the window, and left as silently as he had come. The next morning, the poor man was overjoyed. The gold was more than enough to provide dowries for his three daughters. He praised God for the unknown friend who had come secretly during the night to bring his family these gifts.

Nicholas died around 350 CE, but the memory of this deed lived on. The church called him a saint, and his friends continued delivering gifts to the needy in his name, always secretly at night, with no thought of receiving anything in return. Over the years, this custom spread all over Europe. When people from the Netherlands came to this country, they brought the tradition here. They called the good bishop "San Nicholas," but little children who could not pronounce his name clearly, called him "Sinter Klass." They put out wooden shoes on December 6 for him to fill, never guessing that the gifts were put there secretly by grown-ups who had caught the spirit of the kindly bishop who loved his people and wanted to make them happy.

In 1822, Clement Clark Moore wrote a children's poem about St. Nicholas that changed our picture of him forever. In the poem, the kindly bishop in the red robe becomes a "right jolly old elf" in a fur-trimmed red suit. He rides in a reindeer-drawn sleigh instead of on a horse, and he comes on Christmas Eve instead of December 6. The message is the same, however: God has blessed us with gifts that are meant to be shared cheerfully and in secret with those in need, with no thought of return, for it truly is more blessed to give than to receive.

Prayer: *God, giver of all things, may we too catch the spirit of St. Nicholas, and find joy in playing Santa Claus for those we love and those in need. Amen.*

The Good Queen:
Margaret of Scotland

So if I, your Lord and Teacher, have washed your feet, you also ought to wash one another's feet. For I have set you an example, that you also should do as I have done to you. (John 13:14-15)

I have never been too impressed by royalty. Yet when we were in Scotland in 2005, I found a queen I could respect and admire: Margaret, the shipwrecked Saxon princess who became the second wife of Malcolm, a widowed Celtic king. At Edinburgh castle we saw a small eleventh-century church named after her. We later visited St. Margaret's Church on the Royal Mile. In the sanctuary of that church there was a great blue banner showing Queen Margaret with her arms spread wide, Bible in one hand and cross in the other. The robe across her shoulders sheltered the children in tattered clothing begging at her feet.

I stood looking at that banner for a long time, remembering the stories I had heard about Margaret, "the Good Queen," who was canonized as a saint several hundred years after her death. Until she met Malcolm, Margaret had planned to be a nun. Instead, she became his queen and mother of eight children, whose care and schooling she took on herself, contrary to the customs of the day. Malcolm was devoted to his queen, becoming a better ruler under her influence and supporting her charitable work. Margaret was generous with her time and money in assisting the poor, the aged, the orphans, and the sick. She gave alms to the poor and personally fed large numbers of the hungry before she herself sat down to eat. She encouraged reforms in the church, and brought the Celtic and Roman churches together. She sought to make Sunday a real "Sabbath" day of rest, and influenced people to fast during the forty days of Lent and receive Communion on Easter Sunday. Margaret built churches, providing all the beautiful ornaments required in that time. On the island of Iona, she re-founded St. Columba's monastery, which had fallen into ruins. She established a ferry so pilgrims could visit holy sites more easily, and built places for them to stay and rest. Having studied the Bible from childhood, she delighted in discussing the scriptures with scholars and priests. She regularly fasted and retreated to a nearby cave for prayer and meditation, in addition to offering daily prayers in her church.

My daughter and I spent a week at the abbey on Iona, rooming with two of Margaret's namesakes from the island of Mull. I think the Good Queen would have liked our discipline of prayer, the way we shared in work as well as worship, and our common concern for compassionate justice in the world. I think she would have had much to teach us about following the example of Jesus in laying aside royal robes and serving others. And I'm glad my genealogy research suggests I may be one of her descendants!

Prayer: *God, may we too lay aside our robes of privilege and plenty and put on the humble garb of those who serve your children who are in need. Amen.*

A Living Picture:
St. Francis of Assisi

Jesus, looking at him, loved him and said, "You lack one thing; go, sell what you own and give the money to the poor, and you will have treasure in heaven; then come, follow me." (Mark 10:21)

Francis Bernardone grew up in the little Italian town of Assisi. In his youth, he enjoyed the luxuries he had as the son of a rich man. Then, several illnesses and a year in prison after a skirmish with a neighboring town made Francis question his way of life. *Everyone in the world is fighting over riches,* he thought. *Even the Church and the monasteries are more concerned with money than caring for the needs of their people.*

Francis decided to take Jesus' words to the rich young man seriously. He gave away all his possessions to the poor, and kept nothing beyond the needs of the day. He worked, but accepted no money, only the food and clothing no one else wanted. He went to people where they were—in cities, on farms, in leper colonies, in hospitals, even where Muslims and Christians were fighting over the Holy Land. Everywhere, he joyfully helped the poor and preached the good news about Jesus.

Francis loved Christmas, and it bothered him that, for most people, it was just another day. Few could read the Bible for themselves or understand the Latin scriptures the priests read to them in church. They didn't know the story of how God had come to them in the baby at Bethlehem. How could he make them understand? Then he had an idea. He would give them a living picture of the Christmas story.

Francis knew of a cave at the rear of his churchyard. *It will do for a stable,* he thought, *and I can have the brothers bring in some straw and animals. The young couple down in the village can be Mary and Joseph, and they can lay their own new baby in the manger.*

When Francis led the villagers to the cave on Christmas Eve, they felt as if they were worshiping in Bethlehem itself. But the living picture that made God's love so real to them was not just the manger scene. It was Francis himself, who day after day interpreted that love in words and deeds.

Prayer: *Like St. Francis, Lord, make us instruments of your peace. Where there is hatred, let us sow love; where there is injury, pardon; where there is doubt, faith; where there is despair, hope; where there is darkness, light; and where there is sadness, joy. It is in pardoning that we are pardoned, in forgiving that we ourselves are forgiven, and in producing good will toward others that your peace comes to us. Amen.*
(Prayer of St. Francis)

Embracing the Light

A Model for Today:
St. Birgitta of Sweden

To those who are sanctified in Christ Jesus, called to be saints, together with all those who in every place call on the name of our Lord Jesus Christ, both their Lord and ours... (1 Corinthians 1:2)

In my faith tradition, we do not limit saints to those canonized by the Roman Catholic Church after their deaths. Rather, like the Apostle Paul, we believe that we are all "called to be saints," living saints, set apart by our baptism to worship and serve God according to the way of Jesus Christ. That is why it may seem strange that several years ago our Black Hills United Church of Christ clergy-spouse group met to celebrate All Saints' Day. We each brought a story of our favorite saint to share. Through my genealogy research and travels in Sweden, I had become acquainted with two distant cousins who bore the name of St. Birgitta of Sweden, so I chose to tell about her.

Birgitta (or Bridget) was born early in the fourteenth century to a wealthy landowner, knight, and government official and a pious woman of royal ancestry. Her mother died when she was about twelve, and she was put in care of an equally pious aunt for a year, and then married to a prince named Ulfo. Birgitta became known for her charitable works, especially those that benefited unwed mothers and their children. She also became a lady-in-waiting to the queen.

Birgitta and her prince produced eight children, including a future saint (Catherine), before Ulfo died on a pilgrimage to Santiago de Compostela in Spain. Birgitta, who had begun receiving visions as a child, then gave up her royal title for a life of prayer and caring for the poor and the sick. She was associated with the Franciscan and Cistercian orders, served as counselor and advisor to priests, theologians, and royalty alike, and was not afraid to chasten even popes! She and Catherine made a pilgrimage to Rome, Jerusalem, and Bethlehem. Birgitta stayed in Rome until her death in 1373, continuing her charitable work and attempts to reform corruption in the Church.

Birgitta founded the Birgittine Order in Vadstena, Sweden with the support of Sweden's king. It was a "double monastery," housing monks and nuns in separate cloisters. They were to live simply and give any surplus income to the poor, but could have as many books as they wanted! The monastery is a museum now, but there is a Birgittine house in a Stockholm suburb. Another cousin named after the saint took me there when I was in Sweden in 2014. We saw a statue of St. Birgitta, and her life portrayed in the stained glass windows of the convent chapel. A kindly nun told us how the convent continues the work of this worthy saint and loaded my arms with resources in English about her life. Since then, we have often prayed this prayer of St. Birgitta:

Prayer: *O God, show us your way, and make us happy to follow it. Amen.*

He Came to Serve:
Toyohiko Kagawa

Whoever wishes to be great among you must be your servant, and whoever wishes to be first among you must be your slave; just as the Son of Man came not to be served but to serve, and to give his life a ransom for many. (Matthew 20:26-28)

My husband's parents named him Richard Kagawa Keithahn, and he spent the rest of his life explaining why he had a Japanese middle name! When we were in college, we went to hear Toyohiko Kagawa speak. He was a wizened little man, blind from a disease he had contracted in his work with the poor. His English was hard to understand, but the auditorium was full, a sign of the esteem in which he was held by all those who knew of his work.

Toyohiko Kagawa was born a Buddhist, but an English conversation class led by an American missionary piqued his interest in the Christian faith. A young man in Japan was expected to respect his father and follow his example. However, Toyohiko's father had wasted the family fortune and caused his family a great deal of suffering. His son was looking for someone else to follow, and found him in Jesus.

Like many converts, Toyohiko took his faith seriously. The church members he knew were well off and had little concern for the poor. *Christ came to serve,* he thought, *and I will be a servant too.* He left the seminary where he had studied to be a minister, and went into the slums to live and work among the poor, the sick, the thieves, and the old.

As he became aware of their problems, Toyohiko began to find solutions. He helped factory workers organize labor unions. He collected clothing and supplies for people after Tokyo's great earthquake and fire. He started kindergartens and day nurseries for children whose mothers worked outside the home. He organized agricultural cooperatives and training centers in rural areas. His work became famous not only in Japan but all over the world. He even visited South India where my husband's missionary parents were engaged in similar ministries.

Then World War II began. Always a man of peace, Toyohiko spoke out against the violence being committed by his countrymen and Americans alike. When the war was over, he worked to help the two nations forgive one another and become friends. At the emperor's request, he spoke to him of the Christian faith, sharing with him the principle that had motivated his life: "Whoever would be great among you must be the servant of all."

Toyohiko Kagawa, once ridiculed by well-to-do Christians, did more than any other to influence the character of the Christian churches in Japan. He modeled what Jesus was trying to communicate to his disciples: God has sent me to be your servant, and to enable you to serve one another. Freely you have received of God's love, now freely give it away to all who are in need.

Prayer: *God, may we be like Toyohiko Kagawa, alive with the spirit of Jesus and ready to serve others, even though it may cost us dearly. Amen.*

A Modest Saint:
Forrest Duffield

Now there are varieties of gifts, but the same Spirit; and there are
varieties of services, but the same Lord; and there are varieties of
activities, but it is the same God who activates all of them in everyone.
To each is given the manifestation of the Spirit for the common good.
(1 Corinthians 12:4-7)

It was the summer of 1959 that my husband and I began serving
our first parish in Baker, Montana, a small town located on
U.S. Highway 12 on the eastern edge of the plains of Montana.
Homesteaders had begun settling in the area about 1908, but many
had moved further west during the drought years of the 1930s.
The Duffields were one family that stayed. By the time we arrived,
Jessie Duffield, an elderly widow, and her bachelor son, Forrest,
had finally moved in from their ranch in Fertile Prairie to live in
Baker. They were both in church for every Sunday service.

Forrest, in fact, was an almost indispensable member of the
congregation. He never considered himself educated or able enough
to lead a discussion group or speak in front of people, but whenever
something needed fixing, he was there to make the repairs. When
the trash cans were about to overflow, he emptied them. When the
sidewalks filled with snow, he was there to shovel. Every Sunday
morning he was on hand at the church to greet people by name and
welcome them with a smile. He was a regular usher in worship, not
just on Sundays but for every funeral, too.

Since my husband was always in the pulpit and I sang in the choir, we had to find a place for our children to sit in Sunday worship once they outgrew the church nursery. It was Forrest who had them sit in the back of the sanctuary with him, and help him count the number of worshippers each week. What a gift that was to us!

Whenever anyone praised Forrest for all his good works in the church, he would reply, "When I lived way out on the ranch and was working hard every day, I never was able to get in to church on Sundays. I don't go to church any more than anyone else. I'm just making up for lost time!"

Every congregation needs more "saints" like this modest man!

Prayer: *God, we give you thanks for Forrest and all the other saints like him who find joy in caring so faithfully for the needs of our church family. Amen.*

Two Kinds of Rulers

But [Jesus] said to them, "The kings of the Gentiles lord it over them; and those in authority over them are called benefactors. But not so with you; rather the greatest among you must become like the youngest, and the leader like one who serves. For who is greater, the one who is at the table or the one who serves? Is it not the one at the table? But I am among you as one who serves." (Luke 22:25-27)

When I went to China in 1991 with a tour group, our local guides in Beijing told us that through several dynasties the Chinese people had considered their emperor to be the "Son of Heaven," and thus the center of the universe. In the temple where the emperor offered sacrifices, the square outer wall represented the earth, the round inner wall heaven, and the center point of that circle the emperor. Nine steps led up to that center point, steps only the emperor was allowed to climb. Nine, the highest single digit number, was his number, and no one else could use it. The dragon was the emperor's exclusive symbol, and the color yellow was his alone to use.

The emperor's palace covered 240 acres and was called "The Forbidden City" because ordinary citizens were forbidden to set foot on it. The emperor took 100 of the country's most beautiful young women for his concubines, to serve at his pleasure. His close advisors had to be eunuchs. Castrated men would have no families to distract them, no sons to advance in government. In the emperor's mind, the people of China existed to serve him, and if they did not serve him, they were swiftly punished. "Head off," as our guides often said. The dowager empress had used two years of the national income to build the imperial Summer Palace, now a public lakeside recreational area, but then only used by the royal family. When the emperor wanted to go from the Forbidden City to the Summer Palace, walls of yellow silk were put up along both sides of the road, not so much to screen him from the eyes of the common people, but to keep his eyes from observing their needs, lest he become upset at the sight of people who were hurting, sick, hungry, and poor.

How different was this "Son of Heaven" from the "Son of God" we know, who came to live among us, not apart from us! Born in a manger instead of a palace, he came to share our hunger, our poverty, our sorrows, and our pain, not to be shielded from our needs by a wall of yellow silk. He came not to be served, but to serve, asking no sacrifice he was not willing to make himself. He came to offer us forgiveness, not punishment for our misdeeds. Rejecting the use of force, he used the power of love, love that does not count the cost, does not avoid hard choices, does not fear the cross. If we believe in the reign of Jesus Christ, we can never see the manger without the shadow of the cross, and if we accept his call to be his body in the world, this shadow also falls on us.

Prayer: *We hear Jesus say, "Deny yourselves, take up your cross, and follow me." God, help us to answer "yes." Amen.*

The Shepherd King

I myself will be the shepherd of my sheep....I will seek the lost, and I will bring back the strayed, and I will bind up the injured, and I will strengthen the weak (Ezekiel 34:15-16a)

I am the good shepherd. The good shepherd lays down his life for the sheep. (John 10:11)

Some years ago I was intrigued by a story a guest pastor told us on the last Sunday of the Christian year, a day celebrating the Reign of Christ. She described a church with two beautiful stained glass windows portraying Jesus. One showed the risen Christ as a king, seated on a throne, wearing a crown and holding an orb in one hand and a scepter in the other. The second window pictured the Christ as a shepherd, cradling a lamb in one arm and holding a staff with his other hand. The apparent contradictions between these two images had confused a member of that congregation. "Which one portrays the real Jesus?" she wanted to know.

Which one indeed, I asked myself. Other pictures of Jesus in the Gospels came to mind: Jesus welcoming the children, Jesus treating Zacchaeus as a friend, Jesus healing the sick and helping the blind to see. There is only one answer, I decided, and I went on to write this text that was later set as an anthem for children by Dorothy Christopherson:

We thought a king would wear a crown and sit upon a throne.
He'd hold the world within one hand and call it all his own.
He'd use his scepter to command his subjects to obey,
and they would bow their heads in fear and turn their eyes away.

Yet God sent us a shepherd king to rule with love, not fear;
a shepherd king who gently calls to us, "Come here, come here."
We see the kindness in his eyes, the smile upon his face,
and as he welcomes us, we feel at home in his embrace.

We know if we were lost, alone, or sick and in great pain,
this shepherd king would seek us out to bring us home again,
and whether we were right or wrong, would treat us all the same
because he loves us as his own and knows us each by name.

With alleluias praise our God and bless the holy name
of Jesus Christ, our shepherd king. Forever may Love reign!
May Christ forever rule our hearts, as prophets have foretold,
and may we always find a home secure within his fold.[1]

Prayer: *There are many kinds of power in this world, God. Help us*
         remember that the love of the Good Shepherd is the strongest
         power of all. May it always rule our hearts and lives. Amen.

---

1. Used with Permission. Copyright © 2003 Choristers Guild. CGA970 "The Shepherd King" Dorothy Christopherson, music. Mary Nelson Keithahn, text.

Embracing the Light

OTHER SPECIAL DAYS AND SEASONS

I Resolve

I have loved you with an everlasting love; therefore I have continued my faithfulness to you.…This is the covenant I will make with the house of Israel.…I will put my law within them, and I will write it on their hearts; and I will be their God, and they shall be my people.… I will forgive their iniquity, and remember their sin no more. (Jeremiah 31:3bc, 33-34, sel.)

The beginning of the New Year is a time when many of us make resolutions to change our behavior. We resolve to lose weight. We're going to study harder and get better grades. We're going to try to be a more loving friend. We'll take care of the dog without complaining. But what happens to our resolutions? Our intentions are good, but we just can't seem to keep our promises. Food is too tempting. There are other things to do than study. Our friends try our patience. Taking care of the dog is a real chore.

According to the Bible, God is different. From the time that God made a covenant with the Hebrew people to the time of Jesus, God has resolved to be faithful to us. God has said: I promise to love you. I promise to forgive you when you are sorry for doing wrong things. I promise to help you try harder to be the loving persons I created you to be.

Wonder of wonders, God continues to keep that resolution, no matter what. We may break our promises, but God never does.

What a comfort it is to know we can always count on God's love! That's why we gather to praise God each Sunday.

Prayer: *Thank you, God, for keeping your promise to love and forgive us. Help us to be more faithful in our relationships to you and to one another. Amen.*

A Death on New Year's Day

Do not let your hearts be troubled. Believe in God, believe also in me. In my Father's house there are many dwelling places. If it were not so, would I have told you that I go to prepare a place for you? And if I go to prepare a place for you, I will come again and will take you to myself, that where I am, you may be also. (John 14:1-3)

When a loved one dies on or near a holiday or significant day on the family calendar, that loss is felt anew every time that date rolls around again. I know. My father-in-law died on December 7 (Pearl Harbor Day), my mother-in-law on Mother's Day weekend, my mother just before Thanksgiving, and my father on August 4, his wedding anniversary. My husband died on Memorial Day weekend. Those death anniversaries are easy to remember, and each year are tinged with sadness.

Some years ago I conducted a funeral for an elderly woman who had died on January 1. If she had been born on New Year's Day, the event would have warranted special attention. Business and community groups would have provided her with an assortment of gifts, and pictures of her with her parents would have appeared in the media. People aren't supposed to die on New Year's Day. The new year is ushered in by a smiling baby; it is the old year that creeps away as a weary old man. It is a time to celebrate what is to come, rather than what has passed away, a time when we focus on life rather than death. It is a time to leave behind bad habits, old grudges, and unfulfilled dreams and make a new start in life. But this woman had died on New Year's Day, and there was sadness, not celebration in her family. There would be no new start for her… or would there be?

For Christians, death is as much a symbol for New Year's Day as birth. Death is not the end of life, but a transition, a movement from one stage of life to the next, just as the calendar turns over to a new year. Lucy Montgomery, in her children's book, *Emily of New Moon*,[1] likened death to going through a doorway from one room of life to another. Jesus said, "In my Father's house are many rooms.…I go to prepare a place for you. I will come again and will take you to myself, that where I am you may be also." This woman's life on earth had ended on New Year's Day, but her new life with God was just beginning. So it will be with us when we pass through the curtain of death into our Father's house, with our risen Lord at our side. And that "New Year's Day" will be cause for celebration, not sadness.

Prayer: *In your wisdom, God, you keep us connected to our loved ones by our pain and sadness at their loss. Help us also rejoice that death does not end our lives, but is the beginning of a larger and more abundant life with you. Amen.*

1. Emily of New Moon, *by Lucy Maud Montgomery, first published in 1923.*

Love Letters

You yourselves are our letter, written in our hearts, to be known and read by all; and you show that you are a letter of Christ, prepared by us, written not with ink but with the Spirit of the living God, not on tablets of stone but on tablets of human hearts. (2 Corinthians 3:2-3)

February makes me think of two things: Valentine's Day and birthdays. I was born on February 17, in between the birthdays of two great American presidents.

Both Valentine's Day and birthdays are occasions for sending letters to tell people that we love them. The problem with letters, however, is that they are only words, easy to write or speak, but not really meaningful unless our actions support what we say.

That is what is so wonderful about the "letters" of love God has sent us through the Bible. The Hebrew scriptures are full of God's promises to love and care for us, and God's actions in the lives of the Hebrew people are consistent with that promise. However, it was only when God became one of us in Jesus that we really understood how much God loved us and wanted us to love one another. Jesus was God's letter of love to us. He was a friend to those who had no friend. He helped people who were doing wrong things to change. He forgave those who hurt him. Jesus communicated God's Word in his deeds.

The apostle Paul asks us to think of ourselves as "letters of love" too, letting the Holy Spirit guide our words and deeds so others may know the love of Christ. From now on, when you send Valentines or birthday cards to people you love, don't stop there. Do something more to show them how much you care about them: shovel a walk, invite them for a meal, take them to a concert or a movie, or just spend some quality time together. Be a living "letter of love," supporting your words with your deeds.

Prayer: *God, as you sent Jesus to show us your love in word and deed, send us out to love one another in the same way in his name. Amen.*

"You Gotta Have Heart!"

I will give them one heart, and put a new spirit within them; I will remove the heart of stone from their flesh and give them a heart of flesh, so that they may follow my statutes and keep my ordinances and obey them. (Ezekiel 11:19-20)

I will put my law within them and I will write it on their hearts; and I will be their God, and they shall be my people. (Jeremiah 31:33)

You shall love the Lord your God with all your heart...[and] your neighbor as yourself. (Matthew 22:37-39)

Take heart...your sins are forgiven. (Matthew 9:2)

New Haven, Connecticut, where my husband and I attended Yale Divinity School, was only a few hours away from New York and the Broadway stage. The city was also the home of the Schubert Theater, where many new plays had their first run. Unfortunately, the budget and time constraints of graduate student life limited our theater activity. My husband, for example, missed the opening night of *My Fair Lady* his first year because he had to study for a church history test! However, we did manage to see a few other good shows.

One show we enjoyed was *Damn Yankees*,[1] starring Gwen Verdon. Its Faustian plot has the devil sending a beautiful red-haired dancer to tempt a diehard baseball fan to sell his soul in exchange for a chance to become a baseball hero and lead the faltering Washington Senators to the pennant. In a hit song from the show, team members try to encourage one another in their disastrous season by singing, "You gotta have heart, all you really need is heart, miles and miles and miles of heart…"

I think of this song whenever I read these words from Ezekiel and Jeremiah. These prophets must have had some idea of the heart's physiological function. They knew that when the heart is healthy and strong it gives breath and life to the body; when it fails, the body dies and there are only bones, dry bones, left. However, they also thought of the heart metaphorically as the center of thought processes, the seat of passions, the source of motives, and the spring of conscience. It was the innermost part of one's being that determined the course of one's life, the words that were spoken, and the deeds that were done. The heart was the inner core of a person that could respond to God…or not. The heart could also become wanton and lovesick for other gods, hardened as stone against hearing God's Word and slow to trust and believe, stubbornly set on getting its own way.

Ezekiel and Jeremiah promised that God would give our people one heart, a new heart with the laws of God written on it, laws that Jesus would later sum up as the command to love God and our neighbor, laws that we can only obey when we "take heart" and find the courage to trust in God's gracious, steadfast love.

Prayer: *Create in us a new heart and spirit, God, a heart that bleeds with compassion for the least of your children and understands their needs, and a spirit wise and courageous enough to love and care for them as you care for us. Amen.*

1. *1955 musical comedy with book by George Abbott and Douglass Wallop and music and lyrics by Richard Adler and Jerry Ross.*

Embracing the Light

Mixed Memories
of Mother's Day

I will give thanks to you, O Lord, among the peoples, and I will sing praises to you among the nations. For your steadfast love is higher than the heavens, and your faithfulness reaches to the clouds.
(Psalm 108:3-4)

When life events occur around a holiday, we tend to associate those events with that special day for the rest of our lives. Every holiday celebration brings memories, good and bad, to mind. Mother's Day is one of those holidays for me.

From the time I was eight, I felt my mother's sadness on Mother's Day. It was the custom then for a woman to wear a red flower if her mother were living, and a white flower if she had passed away. My grandmother had died in February, ten days before my birthday, and my mother was wearing a white flower in church that Mother's Day for the first time. As we sat through the service, I could see the tears in her eyes and feel the pain of her loss, and I could do nothing to make her feel better.

Mother's Day has other painful memories for me. There was the Sunday afternoon when an ambulance rushed past our home, siren blowing, on its way to the hospital. We soon learned that a teenage boy who was in high school with our children had been killed in a motorcycle accident. He was the only boy from a large farm family. Some years later, my mother-in-law died on a Mother's Day weekend after what we had thought had been successful surgery. Worst of all for me, my husband had a heart attack on a Mother's Day weekend, and died two weeks later at the age of fifty-two.

Yet I have happier memories associated with this holiday too. Two of my grandchildren were born on Mother's Day, five years apart, and they have brought much joy into my life. There have been other joys around that holiday, as well: music concerts, graduations, travels, and visits from faraway family members.

Events associated with holidays are more easily remembered, but most days on the calendar are like Mother's Day for me, a mixture of happy and unhappy experiences, sorrows and joys, good times and bad. That is the nature of our human existence. As we journey through each year, it is important to remember that God is walking with us each and every day. In joys and in sorrows we are never alone.

Prayer: *Thank you, God, for your faithful, loving presence in our lives, no matter what happens. Amen.*

Embracing the Light

The Best Part

I am reminded of your sincere faith, a faith that lived first in your grandmother Lois and your mother Eunice and now, I am sure, lives in you. (2 Timothy 1:5)

It was Mother's Day and I was responsible for the children's time in worship. When the children came to sit with me in the chancel, I encouraged them to share their plans to do something special with their mothers on this day. Then I told them this story:

Once there was a family that always sat down to Sunday dinner together. Mother would usually cook roast chicken, and Dad would carve and serve the bird at the table. He always let Mother choose what piece of the chicken she wanted first. Mother always answered, "I'll be last, dear, and I like the neck." When the five boys and girls in the family had made their choices, the neck was about all that was left.

The oldest boy wondered if his mother really did like that bony piece of meat, and decided the children should give her another option. He called them together in a secret meeting, and they made a plan. They told their mother that on Mother's Day they would cook dinner for the family, and on Saturday she noticed they were making mysterious trips to the homes of several relatives and next-door neighbors.

On Sunday the whole family went to church together. For once, Mother could worship without worrying about the dinner in the oven. When the family got home, the children finished preparing the food, and they all sat down to dinner. It was roast chicken again. As Dad started to carve the bird, Mother, as usual, said, "I'll be last, and I like the neck." Then Dad asked the children in turn what piece of chicken they wanted. One by one, they replied, "I'd like the neck, please," and Dad put a neck on each plate, including his own! Mother's eyes widened and she finally said, "If I had realized that chicken had seven necks, I would have sold him to a museum!"

"It is a remarkable chicken," Dad agreed, "but there were only six necks. What is your second choice?" Mother laughed, and said, "I'll take a wishbone, please." And everyone cheered!

Afterwards, when the children were cleaning up the kitchen, the oldest said, "You know, Mother always wants the best for us. I wonder if she really did prefer the neck!"

Prayer: *God, who loves us like a parent and created us to live in families, we thank you for loving mothers who want the best for us, and put our needs ahead of their own. Help us to find ways to show them that we love them too. Amen.*

Embracing the Light

The Importance of Remembering

I consider the days of old, and remember the years of long ago.
(Psalm 77:5)

When I was a child, I remember marching, flag in hand, behind the high school band in the parade out to the cemetery on Memorial Day. There we watched veterans place wreaths on graves, covered our ears as the honor guard fired a salute to the dead servicemen, and listened to a trumpeter solemnly play "Taps." We were more serious about Memorial Day during those years of World War II, more certain then that war was God's way of achieving a just peace in the world, more convinced that God was on our side, and our side only.

War is not so glorious when it is taking place in your own country and you are losing a war you started. My sister-in-law was born in an evacuation center outside Munich the year before Germany's defeat. When my son and I visited members of her family in 1989, they recalled lifelong nightmares from the bombings, and surviving on CARE packages and food their mother had bought by selling her valuables, one by one. Everywhere we went there were still reminders of the war: a hilly park constructed from Munich's rubble from over seventy bombing raids, models and photographs of bombed and reconstructed buildings and churches, whole areas of cities destroyed and now restored.

I expressed my sorrow at the part our country had played in such destruction, however necessary it may have been. Our German relatives were surprised at my feelings. "We brought this on ourselves," they said. "War has no winners," I replied. "We all suffer from its effects." But they went on, "Many older Germans want to forget the war and their generation's unwillingness to oppose the Nazi movement. Nothing that happened after 1930 made it into our history books in school. If we do not permit ourselves to remember and learn from the past, how can we avoid mistakes in the future? If we do not recognize the evil we have done and express sorrow for our actions, how can we be forgiven? How can we forgive ourselves?"

Remembering is painful. Memories connect us with past mistakes, suffering, and losses we would rather forget. Yet memories also connect us with the God who has suffered with us and with our enemies, who has wept at the injuries and injustices we have inflicted upon one another, who has forgiven us and helped us to become reconciled, and who inspires us now to work for peaceful solutions to the problems of our world community.

Prayer: *God, we pray that Memorial Day will always be more than a day of relaxation and recreation for us. Let it also be a time of remembering the horrors and ultimate futility of war, and a time of rededicating ourselves to the cause of peace. Amen.*

Rejoice in the Saints

To those who are sanctified in Christ Jesus, called to be saints, together with all those who in every place call on the name of our Lord Jesus Christ, both their Lord and ours: Grace to you and peace from God our Father and the Lord Jesus Christ. (1 Corinthians 1:2b-3)

Thanksgiving has always been one of my favorite holidays. When I was growing up, my family traditionally hosted the Thanksgiving dinner for all of my father's relatives. I had a number of cousins my age, and none of them lived in our town. This was our one chance to be together each year, and it was a happy, noisy occasion. We gave thanks, stuffed ourselves at dinner, helped with dishes, played games, and walked and talked together. The Thanksgiving memories we shared bound us together all our lives.

Thanksgiving has also been important to me as a spiritual descendant of those brave "saints and strangers" who left England to build a new life in this country. When we were serving Pilgrim Congregational United Church of Christ in Benson, Minnesota, we often celebrated the holiday by recreating the lengthy worship style of the Pilgrims. We removed the cross and candles from the chancel, divested the minister and choir of their robes, seated men and boys on one side of the sanctuary and the women and girls on the other, prayed with arms uplifted, lined out metrical psalms for a cappella singing, questioned the preacher after the sermon, and left an offering with the deacons for the poor. We even gave one of the ushers a pole with a feather at one end to tickle a sleepy worshiper awake, and a knob at the other end to discipline unruly parishioners. And one year we bought bolts of fabric and sewed Pilgrim costumes for everyone in the children's choir!

In 1995, my interest in the Pilgrims led me to join a tour group bound for England to explore the history of our spiritual ancestors at sites such as Scrooby, Gainsborough Hall, Boston Guild Hall, Cambridge, Plymouth, and London. As I walked in their footsteps and came to understand the courageous sacrifices they had made for the chance to worship freely in a new land, my heart was filled with gratitude for these saints and the faith they handed down to me. Little did I know then that my genealogy research would later show that eight of the Mayflower passengers also passed on their DNA to me!

Prayer: *God, when we sit down at a bountiful table with our family and friends on Thanksgiving Day, help us to remember to give thanks for the Pilgrim saints whose faith and courage gave us reason to celebrate this day. Amen.*

Be Thankful

O come, let us sing to the Lord; let us make a joyful noise to the rock of our salvation! Let us come into his presence with thanksgiving; let us make a joyful noise to him with songs of praise! (Psalm 95:1-2)

We think of Thanksgiving as an American holiday, rooted in the Hebrew festival of Succoth, but many other peoples and nations around the world also observe a day of thanksgiving in their own time and their own way.

In India, Christians used to hold special services in which church members came forward to place their gifts upon the altar. In cities, where people worked for wages, the gifts were usually money. In rural areas, people were more likely to bring rice or vegetables as their thankofferings.

At one such service, an old widow arrived at the church with an extraordinarily large offering of rice. The pastor, who traveled around to serve many congregations, did not know the widow well, but he did know that she was poor, and the offering was much more than she could afford. He asked her if her offering was made in gratitude for some unusual blessing.

"Yes," the woman replied. "My son was sick and I promised a large gift to God if he got well."

"And your son has recovered?" the pastor asked.

The widow paused. "No," she said. "He died last week. But I know that he is in God's care, and for that I am especially thankful."

It is easy to give thanks on Thanksgiving Day, when we gather around a bountiful table, surrounded by loving family and friends. It is much harder when that table is bare, and we are alone. Yet that is the very time we should feel most grateful, for we know by faith and grace that God is with us, caring for us, even in the darkest moments of our lives.

Prayer: *God, may we treat each new day as an opportunity to give thanks for your presence in our lives. We know that no matter what happens, we are never alone. We are always in your care. Alleluia! Amen.*

Counting Our Blessings

When I was a child, I spoke like a child, I thought like a child, I reasoned like a child; when I became an adult, I put an end to childish ways. (1 Corinthians 13:11)

Canning and freezing fruits and vegetables for winter meals was part of my summer routine when I was planning meals and cooking for our family of six. It was easy to dish out canned peaches and pears, but serving the Bing cherries took a little more effort. My children insisted that they each get the same number of cherries in their bowls! They saw that we served the Sunday apple pie with equal justice, too: The person who cut the pie always received the last piece!

My children are now grown with families of their own. I thought of them the other day when I heard a story about a man who died, leaving his two sons equal shares of his property. One son lived on a hill with his large family. The other son was a bachelor who lived alone in the valley.

One night the bachelor son awoke and said to himself, *My father divided his property equally between us, but was that fair? My brother has a large family and many responsibilities, and here I am without any such obligations. I have more than I need. I know my brother would not accept anything from me, so tonight I will move some of my grain to my brother's barn myself.*

That very same night, up in his house on the hill, the older brother lay awake thinking, *I don't think my father treated my brother and me equally. Here I am with a loving wife and family, and my brother lives down in the valley alone. He has no children to look after him in his old age. I think I'll take some of my grain and leave it in his barn tonight, because I know he would never accept it if I tried to give it to him directly.*

Later that night, the two brothers met halfway between their homes, their arms laden down with sheaves of grain. When each realized what the other was doing, they wept with tears of joyful understanding and love.

The refrain of an old hymn advises us, "Count your blessings, name them one by one; Count your many blessings, see what God has done!" When the brothers in the story counted their blessings, they were not worried about whether they had enough for themselves, but whether they had enough to share with those who had less. They had grown in their faith, and their sense of justice led to generosity, rather than selfishness. May it be so with each of us.

Prayer: *Giver of life and all that is good, fill our hearts with gratitude for our countless blessings from you, and move us to share what we have received with those in need. Amen.*

CHRISTIAN LIFE

God Wants YOU!

Now the word of the Lord came to Jonah son of Amittai, saying, "Go at once to Nineveh, that great city, and cry out against it; for their wickedness has come up before me." But Jonah set out to flee to Tarshish from the presence of the Lord. (Jonah 1:1-3)

One of my memories from growing up during World War II is a military recruitment poster with a picture of Uncle Sam, resplendent in his stars and stripes, pointing his forefinger at me and saying, "Uncle Sam wants YOU!"

Now, I was a girl and under ten, but even I squirmed under Uncle Sam's gaze and that demand. I could only imagine how that poster affected young men who were subject to the draft. Although most of them accepted the inevitability of military service, I suspect they responded to that call with a mixture of loyalty and fear. Probably more than one wished they could run in the opposite direction from that obligation, just as Jonah did when God called on him!

Jonah earned his reputation for trying to avoid answering God's call, but he had good company in the Bible. Moses made all kinds of excuses when God called him to lead the Hebrews out of slavery in Egypt. Elijah ran away to hide in a cave out of fear for his life. He was the last prophet alive and wanted to keep it that way! Jeremiah argued that he was too young to endure being a prophet. Even Jesus looked for a way out from the suffering that lay ahead of him, praying in the Garden, "Father, if you are willing, remove this cup from me." Yet in the end, each one of these men accepted the inevitable and responded as Jesus did, "not my will but yours be done" (Luke 22:42). They gave their lives over to God, and God was with them all.

There was at least one in the Bible who managed to decline God's call, however. Although this young man had carefully followed all the commandments, he could not bring himself to give up what he valued most, his wealth and possessions, in order to follow Jesus. He went away grieving, and disappeared into the crowd, nameless and alone.

When God calls us today, we too have a choice. We can follow the way of love and live in God's presence, or we can turn away sorrowfully and live for ourselves alone. Which will it be?

Prayer: *Take away our excuses and alibis, and forgive our fears and false values, God. Give us courageous hearts and strong wills to answer "Yes" when you call. Amen.*

Never Doubt the
Power of a Song

Be filled with the Spirit, as you sing psalms and hymns and spiritual songs among yourselves, singing and making melody to the Lord in your hearts, giving thanks to God the Father at all times and for everything in the name of our Lord Jesus Christ.
(Ephesians 5:18b-20)

When I was growing up, our youth group at church used to sing a hymn called "To the Knights in the Days of Old."[1] It was about following the light of God's love, as knights long ago had followed their vision of the Holy Grail. The text, written by Helen Hill Miller, had won the Silver Bay Prize at Bryn Mawr College in 1920. The tune was composed in 1915 by Sallie Wood Hume Douglas who practiced her hobbies of song-writing and genealogy in Honolulu and published such other tunes as "Hawaiian Love Song" and "Her Pink Mumu"! The version we sang was in three-four time, harmonized in octave chords, but another version used broken chords in six-eight time. I'm not sure why this somewhat silly text with its "music hall" tune appealed to me. I really didn't know much about King Arthur and the Holy Grail, and I never learned to play tunes like that on my piano, but I loved singing that hymn. I think I was at a time in my life when I was drawn to following the way of Jesus, and when I sang the refrain, "Follow the gleam of the light that shall bring the dawn," I was answering that call.

Another hymn popular at that time evoked a similar response in me. The hymn began "Are Ye Able," said the Master, "to be crucified with me?"[2] The text was written by Earl B. Marlatt (1892-1976), a well-educated university and seminary professor, theologian, prize-winning poet, and hymnal editor. Harry S. Mason (1881-1964), who wrote the tune BEACON HILL, was a seminary organist and teacher. The text was better poetry and based on an event in the life of Jesus, not romantic mythology, and the classical-style tune would never have been heard in a music hall, yet I heard Jesus' call to me in each stanza, and every time we sang the refrain, I was answering that call:

> *Lord, we are able. Our spirits are thine.*
> *Re-mold them, make us, like thee divine.*
> *Thy guiding radiance above us shall be a beacon to God,*
> *to faith and loyalty.*

Never doubt the power of song to stir our spirits and call our hearts to follow the light of God's love as revealed in Jesus the Christ!

Prayer: *God, we thank you for all the songs of our faith that help us hear your call and answer "Yes." Amen.*

---

1. *This hymn was included in* New Worship and Song, *a small hymnal published in 1942 by The Pilgrim Press for use in Sunday schools, youth groups, and summer camps.*

2. *Ibid.*

Take the Plunge

To another [Jesus] said, "Follow me." But he said, "Lord, first let me go and bury my father." But Jesus said to him, "Let the dead bury their own dead; but as for you, go and proclaim the kingdom of God." Another said, "I will follow you, Lord; but let me first say farewell to those at my home." Jesus said to him, "No one who puts a hand to the plow and looks back is fit for the kingdom of God." (Luke 9:59-62)

Evans Plunge in Hot Springs, South Dakota is a long-time favorite for those of us who live in the Black Hills. The gigantic indoor pool is filled with naturally warm (87 degrees Fahrenheit) water flowing in from an enormous thermal spring at a rate of 5000 gallons per minute. Adults may come for these healing waters, but families come to play on the imaginative floats and the huge water slides.

Climbing up to the top of the waterslides made me realize why the pool was named Evans Plunge. Once you mount the ladder, there's no chance to change your mind. You have to risk starting down that slide and plunging in to the waters below.

Being a follower of Jesus is like taking that plunge down the waterslide. Once we commit to following the way of love, there's no turning back. We have to take the risk that the way may not be easy and we might get hurt. We can't say: I'll forgive you once, but never again. I'll be kind to you, if you are kind to me. I'll share, if you share. I'll listen, if you listen. I'll listen once, but I don't have time for more. We have to plunge right in, and try with all our heart and mind and soul to be loving persons, all of the time, to everyone.

Prayer: *God, we want to follow Jesus. Give us the courage we need to plunge into his way of love. Amen.*

Born Again

*Jesus answered him, "Very truly, I tell you, no one can see the kingdom
of God without being born from above." Nicodemus said to him, "How
can anyone be born after having grown old? Can one enter a second
time into the mother's womb and be born?" Jesus answered, "Very
truly, I tell you, no one can enter the kindom of God without being
born of water and Spirit. What is born of the flesh is flesh, and what is
born of the Spirit is spirit." (John 3:3-6)*

Howard Mumma, a Methodist minister, was serving an American
church in Paris in 1950. One day he noticed a man in a dark suit who
was surrounded by admirers at the back of the sanctuary. The man
was Albert Camus, the famous French existentialist. The two men
eventually became close friends. Although there had always been
rumors that Camus was drawn to the Christian faith, he had never
converted. "I have been coming to church because I am seeking,"
he explained one evening. "I'm almost on a pilgrimage—seeking
something to fill the void I am experiencing.…I am searching for
something the world is not giving me."

Camus knew the Bible well, and of all its characters he was most
drawn to Nicodemus. "What does it mean to be born again, to
be saved?" he asked Mumma one day. And Mumma replied, "To
me, to be born again is to enter anew or afresh into the process
of spiritual growth. It is to receive forgiveness, and wipe the slate
clean. It is a readiness to move ahead, to commit yourself to new
life, a new spiritual pilgrimage." Camus looked at him with tears

in his eyes and said, "Howard, I am ready. I want this. This is what I want to commit my life to." Sadly, shortly after this conversation happened, Camus died in a car accident. He had waited too long.[1]

For someone like me, who was baptized as an infant, confirmed her faith at the age of twelve, and was ordained to the ministry at fifty-three, being "born again" has been more of a process than a once and for all conversion experience. I grew up never knowing myself as anything but a Christian, yet I have always been conscious of my failures in living out my faith and my need for God's forgiveness, not once, but over and over again. Each time I lay the wrongs I have done and the good I have left undone before God, I know God forgives me and gives me the will and strength to be more faithful to the way of love. God understands that imperfect backsliders like me need more than one chance. It made me sad to learn Albert Camus did not trust God enough to commit to this process while he still had time.

Prayer: *God of the second chance, and third, and fourth, and more, how grateful I am for your patient, steadfast, forgiving love that has sustained and encouraged me all my life. Amen.*

---

1. *Some years ago, the* Christian Century *magazine reported this incident as having been mentioned in a sermon by the Rev. John Buchanan.*

Embracing the Light

Many Possessions

Jesus, looking at him, loved him and said, "You lack one thing; go, sell what you own, and give the money to the poor, and you will have treasure in heaven; then come, follow me." When he heard this, he was shocked and went away grieving, for he had many possessions. Then Jesus looked around and said to his disciples, "How hard it will be for those who have wealth to enter the kingdom of God!" (Mark 10:21-23)

People in biblical times tended to interpret their economic status as a sign God approved or disapproved of their actions. When they lived according to God's laws, God blessed them with riches. When they turned away from God's laws, God cursed them with poverty.

Jesus looked at economic status not as a result of God's approval or disapproval, but as a help or hindrance in our response to God's love. The story of his encounter with the rich man is a reminder that the more wealth we have, the greater is our temptation to make things more important than God in our lives.

Jesus' insight may sound encouraging to farmers and ranchers who struggle to survive in a series of drought years, or teachers working extra jobs to support their families, or single parents working at minimum wage jobs. Wealth is one problem they don't have! Yet, as serious and heart-breaking as these problems are, as a nation, we are still closer to affluence than the poverty line when we compare ourselves with much of the rest of the world. We are all tempted to put our desire for things ahead of our desire to serve God. We need to be challenged by Jesus' words, not comforted!

Prayer: *Faithful, ever-loving God, you have chosen us to be your people. Help us choose you to be our God, and to put you first in our lives, over and above all the things that tempt us. Amen.*

Can't or Won't?

To another he said, "Follow me." But he said, "Lord, first let me go any bury my father." But Jesus said to him, "Let the dead bury their own dead, but as for you, go and proclaim the kingdom of God." Another said, "I will follow you, Lord; but let me first say farewell to those at my home." Jesus said to him, "No one who puts a hand to the plow and looks back is fit for the kingdom of God." (Luke 9:59-62)

When our two younger children were in elementary school, my husband and I took a course called Parent Effectiveness Training. One of the techniques we learned was called "active listening." This involved listening carefully to what a child was saying so we could restate his or her concern in our own words to show we had understood it. When we tried out the technique at home, it worked well with our youngest, but when we tried it with Stephen, he would look at us quizzically, and say, "Is this some of that Parent Effectiveness Training again?" So much for "active listening" in conversations with him!

Some years later Stephen turned the tables on me. He had just finished his first year at Duke Medical School when his father died. When he did his psychiatric rotation the following fall, he was intrigued by a technique one of the therapists used. Whenever a discouraged patient would say, "Oh, I can't do that…," the therapist would reply, "Can't or won't?" It is an important question. Do we refuse a task because we are really unable to do it? Or, are we just unwilling to try?

My first year of widowhood was difficult, and I often found all the things I had to learn to do for myself overwhelming. I had married right out of college, and had never lived on my own. I was fifty-two years old and had never driven any distance by myself, or even pumped my own gas! Whenever I was faced with a new task and would tearfully tell Stephen, "I can't do that…," he would respond, "Can't or won't?" With his frank prodding, I discovered I could do many things I had never needed to do nor cared to try when my husband was alive, and I could do most of them well (except for pounding a nail in straight!). How much I had missed when I said "I can't" and really meant "I won't!"

Can't or won't? Jesus prodded his would-be disciples in this Gospel story in much the same way when they offered excuses for not following him immediately. Give me an answer, he said. Are you willing to follow me or not? If you are willing, then go and proclaim the kingdom of God! It is the question each of us in the church has to answer for ourselves today.

Prayer: *God, when we hear the call of Jesus to follow him, give us the will to answer "Yes" without excuses or delays. Amen.*

There Is No Fear in Love

God is love, and those who abide in love abide in God, and God abides in them.…There is no fear in love, but perfect love casts out fear; for fear has to do with punishment, and whoever fears has not reached perfection in love. We love because he first loved us.
(1 John 4:16b, 18-19)

When my husband and I were students at Yale Divinity School in New Haven, Connecticut, we lived in student housing on the campus. We had not been there long when the aroma of Indian cooking drew us down the hall to the door of Joseph and Sarala Barnabas. My husband, the son of missionaries, had grown up in India. Joe, a professor of physics at Ahmednagar College, was at the seminary preparing to become the college chaplain and dean of students upon his return to India. Sarala was working on her master's degree in American literature, with the goal of teaching at the college level and becoming a writer. We became lifelong friends. Joe and Sarala were godparents for our first child, and our families have managed to meet several times over the years in India and in the United States.

Joe once told us how his Hindu family had become Christian as a result of an accident with the Hindu god, Ganesh. It seems that his grandfather and his family had been at a party where they had all enjoyed music, plays, and good things to eat. In the midst of the merry-making, someone had dropped a clay statue of Ganesh and broken the elephant-god's trunk. They were all terrified.

Ganesh will be angry at our carelessness, they thought. *He will bring us nothing but bad luck from now on!* Their fears seemed warranted as Joe's grandfather began spending his money on good times and other women, neglecting his wife and children, and blaming all his troubles on Ganesh. Finally he got tired of being afraid, and marched his family off to be baptized by Christians who did not believe in angry elephant-gods!

Joe's father, Ramachandra, was old enough by then to make his own decisions about matters of faith. He took time to study the Bible and talk with the missionaries. He learned that Jesus preached a God of love, who takes away fear, forgives mistakes, and helps us to be kind and loving persons. Ramachandra chose to be baptized, not because it offered magical protection, but because he had truly come to believe in the God of Jesus Christ. He took the Christian name of Nathanael Barnabas, was ordained to the ministry, and taught in a seminary. He raised his sons and daughters as Christians, praying with them every morning and evening. "God is a God of love," he would say. "Fear not." Many years later, as he lay dying, he prayed, "Jesus, if you are with me, I am not afraid."

Prayer: *God, take away the fear pervading our world today that leads us to hate and distrust one another, and so often results in violence. Help us trust in your way of love, as revealed in Jesus Christ, that we may be kind, compassionate, forgiving people of peace. Amen.*

Passing on the Mantle

Now when the Lord was about to take Elijah up to heaven by a whirlwind, Elijah and Elisha were on their way from Gilgal....Then Elijah said to him, "Stay here; for the Lord has sent me to the Jordan." But he said, "As the Lord lives, and as you yourself live, I will not leave you." So the two of them went on....Then Elijah took his mantle and rolled it up, and struck the water; the water was parted to the one side and to the other, until the two of them crossed on dry ground....Elijah ascended in a whirlwind into heaven....[Elisha] picked up the mantle of Elijah that had fallen from him, and went back and stood on the bank of the Jordan...."The spirit of Elijah rests on Elisha."
(2 Kings 2:1-15, sel.)

When I was in Jordan with a group of church leaders in 2004, we stood on Elijah's hill where, according to widely accepted tradition, the events in this story took place. We recalled how Elijah had given his mantle to Elisha, authorizing him for ministry; and how a chariot and horses of fire had separated them before Elijah was swept up to heaven in a whirlwind. Then a church musician in our group started singing in her rich voice, "Swing Low, Sweet Chariot," and we all joined in. It was a sacred moment in a sacred place.

The story of Elijah's passing on his mantle to Elisha has an even more personal meaning for me, however. I was a minister's wife for almost thirty years. My husband and I had gone to college and seminary together, and we had served churches in Montana and

Minnesota before coming to South Dakota. We had always worked as a team, but I had never been ordained. We were committed to serving rural and small town churches that could afford only one staff member, so I had worked as a volunteer, mainly in the area of Christian education and music. When my husband died in 1986, I heard God calling me, not just in my own heart, but in the voices of colleagues and friends, to carry on his ministry. I applied for ordination, and was ordained the next year. A colleague from our Minnesota years gave the charge to me as a new pastor. Knowing that I had had my husband's robes altered to fit me, he used the story of Elijah's passing on his mantle to Elisha in his remarks. Ordination had authorized me for ministry, he said, but I was not my husband, and I would have to find my own way of being true to my calling, just as Elisha had done.

For ministers, wearing a robe is a sign of our calling. It is not a license to "do our own thing." Although our particular gifts and personalities and the situations that confront us influence our approach to ministry, we are always called to act within the parameters of our faith: the biblical story of God's people, the history and traditions of our faith community, and the words we hear God speaking to us today. From the time my husband's mantle of leadership was passed on to me, I have tried to be faithful to that call.

Prayer: *God of strength and hope, bless all of us who receive the mantle of leadership in the church with the courage of Elijah to confront evil with your words of truth, and the compassion of Elisha to care for our neighbors with love. Amen.*

Mitakuye Oyasin:
All My Relatives

*For as in one body we have many members, and not all the members
have the same function, so we, who are many, are one body in Christ,
and individually we are members one of another....Love one another
with mutual affection; outdo one another in showing honor....Rejoice
in hope, be patient in suffering, persevere in prayer. Contribute to the
needs of the saints; extend hospitality to strangers....Live in harmony
with one another....Live peaceably with all.*
(Romans 12:4-5, 9-18, sel.)

Mitakuye Oyasin! We are all relatives.

Living in the Black Hills of South Dakota for several decades has
given me an opportunity to become acquainted with the spiritual
beliefs of the Lakota people. I have been struck by the way some
of their ideas parallel my own beliefs as a Christian. For example,
the Lakota people often use the phrase "Mitakuye Oyasin," which
can be translated as "All My Relatives." It is used as a greeting, and
at the beginning and end of prayers. The phrase affirms their faith
that the world is one extended family encompassing Grandfather or
Great Spirit, Mother Earth, and all their relatives: the four-legged,
the two-legged, those that fly and those that swim, even those that
are inanimate like rocks and water. All things, all creatures, and all
people are interrelated and interdependent. What happens to one
member of this extended family affects everyone, and all share a
mutual responsibility in caring for one another.

This is evident in the Lakota view of the family. For the Lakota people, a "family" is not just the nuclear family of biological parents and children. The "tiyospaye" or family circle literally includes "all their relatives"—grandparents, aunts and uncles, cousins, and all those incorporated into the family through marriage. The Lakotas even have an elaborate ceremony for making friends into relatives, so they are treated like family too. The ceremony reminds everyone of what relatives are expected to do for one another: feed those who are hungry, clothe those who are naked, help those who are in need.

To a Christian like me, this all sounds very familiar. We too think of ourselves as members of an extended family, the family of God. God has "made us relatives" through our baptism, and called us to live as "brothers and sisters in Christ," serving and caring for one another and the world God has given us to share.

What a difference it could make if we would always greet one another with "Mitakuye Oyasin," and remind ourselves at the beginning and end of our prayers that we are all members of one family!

Prayer: *Tunkashila, Grandfather, who has created us all to live together on Mother Earth, open our eyes that we may see one another as members of one family, bound together by our love for you. Mitakuye Oyasin! Amen.*

Telling Their Stories

Therefore, since we are surrounded by so great a cloud of witnesses, let us also lay aside every weight and the sin that clings so closely, and let us run with perseverance the race that is set before us, looking to Jesus the pioneer and perfecter of our faith, who for the sake of the joy that was set before him endured the cross, disregarding its shame, and has taken his seat at the right hand of the throne of God.
(Hebrews 12:1-2)

At the time of my ordination to the ministry, several friends gave me beautiful handmade stoles to wear with my pulpit robe. One was woven in my favorite rainbow colors, suitable for any of the liturgical seasons, and the other was embroidered in white and gold for use on Christmas and Easter. I like to wear stoles because they remind me of the yoke of service that I accepted when I was ordained.

Some time ago, I came across a pattern for a quilt based on symbols for some of the women mentioned in the Bible. *How appropriate it would be for a female pastor to wear a stole that incorporated symbols for the faithful women who have gone before us,* I thought. However, after trying unsuccessfully to reduce the pattern pieces to a size small enough for a stole, I decided I would make a quilt instead. It would be a scrap quilt, constructed from hand-sewn twelve-inch appliqued and embroidered blocks pieced together from fabrics in many different colors and designs. Each block would represent a woman from the Bible, and I could use the quilt to tell their stories to children in worship or to other groups.

When I started listing the women I found in the Bible, I had many more names to include than the twelve mentioned in the quilt pattern book. In fact, I found so many that I ended up making two quilts, one for women in the Hebrew scriptures and one for women in the New Testament, each with twenty-five blocks! I used the patterns in the quilt book, and found other ideas for designs in symbol and banner books and in the stories themselves. My granddaughter designed one block for me, and my daughter trimmed the blocks to uniform size, and machine-stitched them together within a dark green latticework. I hand-quilted both quilts, adding more names in the latticework, and sewed on the binding. Once I finished these quilts, I started another, this time featuring women from church history.

The blocks in my quilts remind me that I am only one in a long line of women who have been called to accept the yoke of serving God, each in her own way, according to her unique and special gifts. I am humbled by their lives, even as I am encouraged by their faith and perseverance. When I die, I want these quilts to drape my casket, just as a stole would have draped my pulpit robe. I will have "finished my race" and joined the faithful women in that "great cloud of witnesses" surrounding us, and it will then be time for others to remember us and tell our stories.

Prayer: *God, we give you thanks for all the women who are our ancestors in faith, and for all the ways they have inspired our own commitment to your way of love. May each new generation continue to explore new and creative ways to tell their stories as part of our heritage of faith. Amen.*

What's In A Name?

A woman named Martha welcomed [Jesus] into her home. She had a sister named Mary, who sat at the Lord's feet and listened to what he was saying. But Martha was distracted by her many tasks; so she came to him and asked, "Lord, do you not care that my sister has left me to do all the work by myself? Tell her then to help me." But the Lord answered her, "Martha, Martha, you are worried and distracted by many things; there is need of only one thing. Mary has chosen the better part, which will not be taken away from her." (Luke 10:38-42)

One thing each of us has is a name. Usually it is one our parents have given us at birth. Perhaps they named us for a beloved family member or friend they wanted to honor or remember, or a great person whose qualities they hoped we would imitate. Perhaps they gave us a name no one else had because they wanted us to be unique.

My parents named me "Mary" after one of my grandmothers and my father's favorite high school English teacher. I've always liked my name, except for a few childhood years when for some strange reason I wished I had been called "Joan." I've liked my name because it reminded me of all the Marys in the Bible. There was Mary, the mother of Jesus, of course, and Mary Magdalene and the other Mary at the tomb. But the Mary with whom I identified most was Mary of Bethany, the sister of Martha and Lazarus, and a good friend of Jesus. Mary and her family often entertained Jesus in their home, and Mary would sit and listen to Jesus by the hour, often to the exasperation of Martha, who would be bustling about trying to get dinner on the table. Jesus chided Martha when she complained about Mary, and told her, "There is need of only one thing. Mary has chosen the better part, which will not be taken away from her."

When I was confirmed as a seventh grader, our minister gave each of us a watchword from the Bible to carry with us in life. My verse included Jesus' words of encouragement to Mary. Seeking out the presence of Christ, listening to his words, and learning from him has shaped my life these many years since. When I was in Israel in 1996, I was able to visit the church in Bethany that honors Mary and her family, and there I gave thanks for her friendship with Jesus and the inquiring faith she had modeled for all of us named Mary.

Prayer: *God of many names, when we are tempted to let the demands of everyday life dominate our time and energy, help us remember Mary of Bethany who let her work go lest she miss her chance to listen and learn from Jesus. May we be her namesake in spirit, as well as in fact, and follow her example. Amen.*

Sharing the Bread

The Lord Jesus on the night when he was betrayed took a loaf of bread, and when he had given thanks, he broke it and said, "This is my body that is for you. Do this in remembrance of me."
(1 Corinthians 11:23b-24)

The home of the Iona Community is an island two miles wide and five miles long, situated in the Hebrides off the west coast of Scotland. This was where St. Columba established a Celtic monastery in the sixth century, and the Roman church built a Benedictine abbey and Augustinian nunnery in the twelfth century. The place fell into ruins after the Reformation, but during World War II, Scottish Presbyterians began restoring the abbey and developing the grounds for a new ecumenical movement they called the Iona Community. The Community has members from all major Christian traditions in the United Kingdom and beyond, and associate members throughout the world. They follow a discipline of prayer and generosity, and work for social justice and peace wherever they live, meeting together on Iona when they can for rest and renewal.

In the week we spent living in the abbey, we shared in the work that sustained the Community and the discipline of worship at regular intervals throughout each day. The music, drama, art, and symbolic actions of our worship helped us look at the Bible and our faith in new ways, and encouraged us to renew our commitment to justice and peace. Even the Sacrament of Communion was cause for reflection. Jesus had taken bread at his last supper with his friends, divided it so there was enough for all, and shared it with everyone at the table. He had told them, "Do this in remembrance of me," and no matter what our tradition, all of us in that abbey had celebrated this meal regularly. But what if Jesus had something more in mind for his friends to do than simply replicating the last meal they had shared? What if Jesus had intended us to see that the sharing of bread in his name was as important as the meal itself?

George MacLeod, founder of the Iona Community, once said, "The great community problem of our modern world is how to share the bread." MacLeod, of course, was using "bread" as a symbol for all that we need to live—food, clothing, shelter, jobs, health care, education. Jesus seemed to understand bread in the same way when he prayed "Give us this day our daily bread" with his friends. Was he thinking of that symbolic meaning of bread at his last supper? Was sharing all the gifts we need to live with one another the real sacramental act?

Prayer: *Generous and loving God, Giver of all our daily bread, grant that each time we gather at the table for Communion we may hear Jesus' call to share that gift with others in his name. Amen.*

Breaking Bread
with Our Neighbors

The bread that we break, is it not a sharing in the body of Christ? Because there is one bread, we who are many are one body, for we all partake of the one bread. (1 Corinthians 10:16b-17)

In our congregation, on the first Sunday in October each year, we celebrate World Communion Sunday with other Christians around the world. On this day, around the clock for twenty-four hours, some group of Christians somewhere on this planet is breaking bread and sharing the cup in remembrance of Jesus.

On this day in our congregation, however, there is not one bread, but many to feed us. There is whole wheat bread, made from grain grown here in South Dakota, reminding us of the farmers and millers and grocers who have provided it. There is the simple white bread of the poor who struggle to survive among us. There is the fry bread of the Lakota people who were here on this land before the rest of us. There is the cornbread of the American South, and the tostadas of the Central and South Americans, reminding us of the many different places in this hemisphere where Communion is celebrated on this day. There are rice cakes from Asian countries, and dark, strong-flavored rye bread from Europe. And there are pita breads from the Mediterranean areas where our faith began, and unleavened matzohs that link us to our Jewish forbears. The breads we break and share remind us that the body of Christ includes people near and far.

Many breads from many different peoples! But what happened to Paul's affirmation of "one bread, one body"? In a way, our liturgy on this Sunday is like playing a videotape in reverse! It's as if we are sending people away from our Communion table back to their origins in far away places! Yet, isn't that just what World Communion Sunday celebrates? No matter who we are or where we live, our congregation is just one part of the broken body of Christ that our breads represent. It is our prayer on this day that even as this broken bread was scattered, thanks in part to the work of Paul and his successors, it may be gathered up from the ends of the earth and become one body again, with each part sharing its unique gifts with the whole.

Prayer: *God, on this World Communion Sunday, even as we affirm the rich diversity of our brothers and sisters in Christ, we pray that you will heal all that divides us and make us whole, one bread and one body of Christ. Amen.*

Embracing the Light

A Real Spiritual Experience

Beware of practicing your piety before others in order to be seen by them; for then you have no reward from your Father in heaven.
(Matthew 6:1)

In 1633, after months of suffering from the Thirty Years' War and the plague, the townspeople of Oberammergau in Bavaria, Germany vowed to reenact the suffering, death, and resurrection of Jesus Christ every tenth year. The next year they performed their Passion Play for the first time on a stage they had built over the fresh graves of plague victims. From that time, once in every decade, from the middle of May to early October, a costumed cast of local actors and singers performs the Passion Play. The play is now staged in a huge, modern auditorium in Oberammergau. The cast is accompanied by an orchestra playing a musical score composed in 1820. People come from all over the world to watch this play that lasts over eight hours, with a three-hour intermission.

In 2000, my oldest granddaughter Katie, then twelve, and I joined a tour that included a performance of the Passion Play at Oberammergau, along with time in Vienna and Salzburg in Austria and Strasbourg and Paris in France. We had already attended a shorter version of the Oberammergau Play in our neighboring town of Spearfish, South Dakota, and looked forward to experiencing the "real" thing. Since there weren't enough hotels to hold all the visitors in Oberammergau for the play, our tour group was housed in nearby Ettal. Our hotel was not far from the large, castle-like grounds of the Benedictine monastery where there was a beautiful Baroque-style church. After dark, Katie and I walked over to see the church. There were worshippers inside, celebrating the Ascension of Mary. People came out carrying lighted candles and stood singing on the perimeter of the square in front of the church. That gave us an opportunity to go into the sanctuary. The gold and white interior gleamed in the candlelight as we sat there quietly, still listening to the music through the open door. Suddenly the sanctuary flooded with brilliant electric light, and people started coming back inside. We left to make room for them, and went back to our hotel, but for a few moments we felt we had worshiped there too.

The next day we went to Oberammergau for the Passion Play. We sat for four hours, watching the story unfold through the crucifixion, before we had a three-hour break for lunch and shopping. Then we went back to the auditorium to watch the Resurrection scenes. Reenacting the Passion of Christ may well be a spiritual experience for the people of Oberammergau, but a three-hour lunch and shopping intermission between the crucifixion and resurrection blunted its effect on me. What we experienced in the monastery church at Ettal the night before was the "real" spiritual experience for me.

Prayer: *Thank you, God, for those surprising moments when we feel your presence in unexpected places. Amen.*

A Time to Lament,
A Time to Praise

How long must I bear pain in my soul, and have sorrow in my heart all day long? How long shall my enemy be exalted over me?...But I trusted in your steadfast love; my heart shall rejoice in your salvation. I will sing to the Lord, because he has dealt bountifully with me. (Psalm 13:2, 5-6)

Even though I walk through the darkest valley, I fear no evil; for you are with me; your rod and your staff—they comfort me. (Psalm 23:4a)

Sometimes pastors and other worship planners forget that people who live with pain and suffering find it difficult to join the congregation in singing God's praises. Those who are dealing with a life-threatening illness or the loss of loved ones may feel more like voicing their laments and complaints. They need assurance that God accepts these feelings and walks with them in their pain. Knowing they do not face their troubles alone can give them a reason to join in songs of praise even in the worst of circumstances. Psalms 13 and 23 are two biblical examples of this progression from lament to praise.

One summer when I was visiting my son and daughter-in-law in Minnesota, we walked in the Relay for Life, a fundraiser held by the American Cancer Society in their area. We also worshipped with cancer survivors, families of lost loved ones, and people still dealing with the disease. I tried to put myself in their place as I listed to a meditation by one of the area pastors, and came away feeling that his well-intentioned words had not really addressed their needs. That night, when I had returned from this event, I wrote this hymn text:

When we are called to sing your praise with hearts so filled with pain,
that we would rather sit and weep or stand up to complain,
remind us God, you understand the burdens that we bear;
you too have walked the shadowed way and known our deep despair.

When we are called to sing your praise and cannot find our voice,
because our losses leave us now no reason to rejoice,
remind us, God, that you accept our sad laments in prayer;
you too have walked the shadowed way and known our deep despair.

When we are called to sing your praise and life ahead looks grim,
still give us faith and hope enough to break forth in a hymn,
a thankful hymn, great God of Love, that you are everywhere;
you walk the shadowed way with us, and keep us in your care.[1]

After the attack on the United States on September 11, 2001, the United Methodist Publishing House offered this hymn, set to KINGSFOLD, to churches that asked for something to sing the following Sunday. It has since been sung after other tragedies and at funerals, when people have needed a time to sing laments as well as songs of praise.

Prayer: *God, you understand our need to lament before we can sing*
your praise. Help us to accept and honor this need in our
worship too. Amen.

1: © 2000, *Abingdon Press. Used by permission. All rights reserved. The hymn is included in hymnal supplements* The Faith We Sing *(Abingdon Press, 2000) and* Sing The Faith *(Geneva Press, 2003) and the hymnal* Community of Christ Sings *(Herald Publishing House, 2013).*

Cheerful Giving

*Each of you must give as you have made up your mind, not reluctantly
or under compulsion, for God loves a cheerful giver. And God is able
to provide you with every blessing in abundance, so that by always
having enough of everything, you may share abundantly in every good
work.* (2 Corinthians 9:7-8)

When our children began participating in worship with us as a
family or as part of the children's choir, they soon learned that
there were times to stand up and sit down, listen quietly, sing, pray,
and contribute to the offering. There weren't many times to laugh,
however...except one summer Sunday when the Covenant Players
came to lead our worship. A touring troupe from this professional
theater company provided dramatic skits for every part of the
service. The skits were cleverly written with uncommon and often
humorous insight into the nature of the church.

My husband was helping the Covenant Players with the service,
so I was sitting in the midst of the congregation with our four
children. We felt it was important for them to learn to be good
stewards, so when it came time for the offering, I passed out a
quarter to each child, as usual. As the children held on tightly to
their quarters, waiting for the ushers to pass the offering plates,
the Covenant Players began their skit. Each actor assumed the
role of a family member at the Sunday dinner table, and each one
complained about the service they had just attended. "The organ
was too loud." "The sermon was boring." "The room was too hot."

"I didn't like that last hymn." It went on and on until the youngest in the family spoke up. "Well, what do you expect for a quarter?"

There was a joyful noise in the congregation that day as everyone got the point, but no one laughed more than I, as I looked at my children, sitting beside me, still clutching their quarters! But the laughter did not come from being the "cheerful givers" Paul mentioned in his letter to the Corinthians. It was the laughter of embarrassment that we had not brought more to give.

The real joy that leads to cheerful giving is our joy that God has blessed us with more than enough to share in a world where so many are in need.

Prayer: *God, giver of all good things, whether we are rich or poor,*
          may we always find joy in sharing what we have with those
          who have less. Amen.

Saved by Faith

There is nothing love cannot face; there is no limit to its faith; its hope, and its endurance. (1 Corinthians 13:7, New English Bible)

When we visited missionaries Armin and Evelyn Kroehler in Aizu-Takada, Japan, they told us that Evelyn's parents had been missionaries in Japan for many years. Her father felt God had helped him touch many lives through the Christian rural center he had worked so hard to develop. In the months preceding December 7, 1941, however, he feared for both his friends in Japan and his friends in the United States. He could see that the military leaders of Japan seemed bent on using war to extend their empire. He had been warned to return to the United States before it became involved in the conflict, but he would not leave so long as there was any chance to work for peace.

When news came that the Japanese had bombed Pearl Harbor, Evelyn's family was placed under house arrest, and her father was put in solitary confinement while the authorities tried to prove he was an American spy. For six months, he lived alone in a cell, unable to communicate with his family or anyone else in the outside world. The only thing that sustained him during those long, lonely months was his faith in the power of God's love. He drew upon the resources of that faith, long a part of him, as he recited passages from the Bible, sang hymns, and prayed aloud. Unknown to him, his Japanese co-worker, arrested and isolated at the same time, listened to his voice and drew strength from his faith.

Some men, out of concern for themselves or their family, might have given the authorities the confession they wanted. Others might have broken down out of fear, or given themselves over to bitterness and hatred for their captors. But Evelyn's father was saved from these temptations by his unwavering faith in the love of God. Like Jesus, he was well versed in the Scriptures that testified to God's love for him. Hours of prayer and meditation had convinced him that God's love would never fail him. Songs of faith were on his lips and in his heart. He endured his captivity, and lived to serve again as a missionary when the war was over.

Prayer: *May we also strengthen our faith in you, God, through scripture and prayer and song, that we may always trust in your love, no matter what befalls us. Amen.*

Embracing the Light

Moving Mountains

For truly I tell you, if you have faith the size of a mustard seed, you will say to this mountain, "Move from here to there," and it will move; and nothing will be impossible for you. (Matthew 17:20)

When Jesus spoke about "moving mountains," he was using a phrase that was familiar to the Jews. Great teachers who could explain and interpret scripture were often called "uprooters" or even "pulverizers" of mountains, because they were able to remove difficult barriers to understanding God's Word. Jesus used this analogy to emphasize that faith in God's goodness and love is the means by which we can overcome the difficulties that we encounter along life's path.

Sometimes, however, the difficulties we face seem insurmountable. We lose a beloved husband in the prime of life. We are forced to sell our ranch and start over again at a new job. We discover our children are experimenting with drugs or flunking out of school. How do we find and nurture that mustard seed of faith so it can uproot and move the mountains of difficulties that overwhelm us?

Actress Deborah Kerr gave one answer in a newspaper interview during the filming of the movie *Quo Vadis*. A reporter asked if she had been afraid when the lions rushed at her when she was tied to a stake in the Roman Colosseum. She replied, "No, I always read the whole script before I start a movie. I had read to the end, and I knew Robert Taylor would come and rescue me."

Christians are people who have "read to the end of the script." We know that after the cross came the resurrection; after death, life; after suffering, joy. We trust that when we face mountains of difficulties, our God of love will provide for us in the same way. As we share that good news with one another, we find courage to face the future with hope.

Prayer: *Eternal God, our refuge and strength in time of trouble, and our source of understanding in times of perplexity and doubt, help us to put our trust in you, that we might find comfort, courage, and hope in your love. Amen.*

Embracing the Light

When Life Becomes
A Nightmare

My God, my God, why have you forsaken me? (Psalm 22:1a)

But the steadfast love of the Lord is from everlasting to everlasting. (Psalm 101:17a)

Do not be overcome by evil, but overcome evil with good. (Romans 12:21)

(See also Psalms 103 and 121, Micah 6:8, Luke 15:1-10, Genesis 45:5-8.)

The Black Hills, where I live, are located in the Mountain Time Zone. On the morning of September 11, 2001, I was startled awake by the news on South Dakota Public Radio that a plane had just hit the World Trade center in New York. I ran to turn on the television set, and watched the second attack there and on the Pentagon in Washington, DC with horror. Then came news of the fourth plane and the courageous passengers who lost their lives preventing a fourth attack. Like most Americans, I was glued to the television set all day, watching the buildings fall and hearing the stories of the brave rescue workers who lost their lives trying to save victims. I was only seven years old when Japan attacked Hawaii, too young to understand that terror. This was different. I could sense the disbelief and fear that was sweeping the nation. Would we ever feel safe again?

Soon after the attack, Choristers Guild asked composer John Horman and me to write an anthem for children to sing in response to this tragedy. With the horrors of that event indelibly imprinted on our minds, we decided that the text should begin with a lament, in the tradition of the Psalms, and then move to an affirmation of God's compassion and care for us, and God's grief over the choices the attackers had made. It should end with a profession of faith that God can bring something good out of even the worst possible circumstances. Within a few days I wrote this text, John composed a tune, and Choristers Guild published the anthem under the title "We Know Our God Is Faithful."[1]

Prayer: *When life becomes a nightmare that will not go away,*
and evil seems to triumph, and hatred rules the day,
we cry to God in anger, in fear and deep despair:
How can you let this happen while we are in your care?

We know our God is faithful, and slumbers not nor sleeps.
God hears our prayers of anguish. God mourns with us,
and weeps.
God grieves that evil-doers, rejecting love's sweet song,
would stray from paths of justice and choose a way so wrong.

Yet good can come from evil, by reason of God's grace,
and love can calm the nightmares that we have had to face.
As neighbors help a stranger, and others save a friend,
we share the cost of kindness, one family to life's end.

---

1. Used with Permission. Copyright © 2001 Choristers Guild. CGA937 "We Know Our God is Faithful" John D. Horman, music. Mary Nelson Keithahn, text. This text was one of twelve hymns selected for "Songs of Remembrance: Hymns for the Commemoration of September 11, 2001," in a special insert in the July 2002 issue of The Hymn, *journal of the Hymn Society in the United States and Canada. Suggested hymn tune: AURELIA. We pray that it will not have frequent use!*

Embracing the Light

Take Courage

The king of Egypt said to the Hebrew midwives, one of whom was named Shiphrah and the other Puah, "When you act as midwives to the Hebrew women, and see them on the birthstool, if it is a boy, kill him; but if it is a girl, she shall live." But the midwives feared God; they did not do as the king of Egypt commanded them, but they let the boys live....When she could hide him no longer she got a papyrus basket for him, and plastered it with bitumen and pitch; she put the child in it and placed it among the reeds on the bank of the river. His sister stood at a distance, to see what would happen to him. The daughter of Pharaoh...saw the basket among the reeds...."This must be one of the Hebrews' children," she said....She took him as her son. She named him Moses. (Exodus 1:15-2:10, sel.)

When I first heard this story about Moses as a baby, I was a preschooler in Sunday School, and I looked at the event through the eyes of a child. I lived in Minnesota, and I knew about the reeds and rushes that grew on the sides of lakes and rivers. What kind of mother would abandon her baby in a place like that? And in a paper boat? Poor Moses. I was relieved when Pharaoh's daughter found him and took him home.

It was not until I revisited the story as an adult that I realized that there was more to it than I had thought. As a child, I had focused on the baby's plight, without understanding the situation that had put him in danger, or the amount of courage it had taken for the midwives, Shiphrah and Puah, to save his life. As a child, I had not understood the sacrificial love of Jochebed, nor the steadfast loyalty of Miriam, nor the compassion of the Egyptian princess who collaborated with them in saving a Hebrew baby boy. It was only when I looked at the story again through the eyes of mature faith that I realized what these amazing women had done. They had refused to succumb to fear and intimidation, and had found the courage and resourcefulness to resist a powerful ruler and his evil plans. At great risk to themselves, they had chosen to serve the God of the Hebrews instead of Pharaoh. And in so doing, they had saved the person God would call to lead the Hebrews out of Egypt to the Promised Land.

We who have lived in a climate of fear in the United States since we were attacked on September 11, 2001, can take courage from the five women in this story. Their actions show us that the only one we need to fear is God, because it is God who is in charge of this world and all its peoples. God is the one we can trust to love and care for us. God is the one we need to please with our words and deeds, our choices and decisions. God is the one who can inspire in us a will that resists evil, a love that is unselfish, a loyalty that is patient and true, and a compassion that is generous and gracious. If we but trust in that God to guide us, we can live in our world today without being afraid. We can find the courage to resist the powers of evil and do what is good and right in God's sight. We can live in the light of our faith, rather than the darkness of our fears.

Prayer: *Whenever we are afraid, God, help us trust in your love, for that is how we find the courage to do what is right and good in your sight. Amen.*

Embracing the Light

Faith Is Patience in the Night

Now faith is the assurance of things hoped for, the conviction of things not seen....He has said, "I will never leave you or forsake you." So we can say with confidence, "The Lord is my helper; I will not be afraid. What can anyone do to me?" (Hebrews 11:1, 13:5b-6)

I believe that I shall see the goodness of the Lord in the land of the living. Wait for the Lord; be strong, and let your heart take courage; wait for the Lord! (Psalm 27:13-14)

When you pass through the waters, I will be with you; and through the rivers, they shall not overwhelm you; when you walk through fire you shall not be burned, and the flame shall not consume you....Do not fear, for I am with you. (Isaiah 43:2, 5a)

The fruit of the Spirit is love, joy, peace, patience, kindness, generosity, faithfulness, gentleness, and self-control. (Galatians 5:22-23)

My son-in-law was diagnosed with diabetes when he was in college, and by February 1996 had lost the use of his kidneys. Despite having to undergo peritoneal dialysis four times a day during his long wait for a kidney and pancreas transplant, Daryl maintained a positive, hopeful attitude and as active a schedule as his strength allowed. His courage and faith moved me to write this hymn, which was sung to John Horman's new tune for the first time at a healing service for Daryl in his church in September 1998.

Faith is patience in the night, waiting for the morning light,
never giving up the fight.
Spirit God, give us faith.

Faith is laughter in our pain, joy in pleasures that remain,
trust in one we can't explain.
Spirit God, give us faith.

Faith is burning will to live, standing firm and positive,
being ready still to give.
Spirit God, give us faith.

Faith is courage under stress, confidence in hopelessness,
greatest gift we can possess.
Spirit God, give us faith.[1]

When Daryl received the good news in 2000 that donor organs in Denver were a match for him, he took this hymn along when he went to the hospital there. His transplant was successful and he made a fine recovery. For two years he was free to live a more normal life, go back to work full time, and travel with my daughter and their two children. Then, suddenly, he developed a transplant-related lymphoma and died less than two months later on April 11, 2002, at the age of fifty-two. My daughter Becky, ten years his junior, was left with Katie, fourteen and Kenny, nine, to raise alone. It was time for us all to sing the hymn that had comforted Daryl, and pray that God would grant us his faith and courage in the days and years ahead.

Prayer: *Spirit God, give us faith. Amen.*

1. © *Abingdon Press, 2000. Used by permission. All rights reserved. This hymn is included in the hymnal supplements,* The Faith We Sing *(Abingdon Press, 2000) and* Sing The Faith *(Geneva Press, 2003).*

Embracing the Light

For Whom the Bell Tolls

Our years come to an end like a sigh....They are soon gone, and we fly away. (Psalm 90:9b, 10d)

We will all be changed, in a moment, in the twinkling of an eye, at the last trumpet. For the trumpet will sound, and the dead will be raised imperishable, and we will be changed. (1 Corinthians 15:51b-52)

When I was growing up in a small town in southern Minnesota, several of the churches still followed the custom of tolling the church bell whenever a church member had died. The bell would first be rung freely to signal a death, and then tolled slowly, one ring for each year in the life of the deceased. We would all stop what we were doing and listen, counting the rings as the bell tolled and wondering aloud who had died this time. Then the bell would be rung freely again, and we would all go about our business. Death was, after all, something that usually happened to someone else.

It was not until I was a young woman in seminary, married, and the mother of one child, that it suddenly occurred to me that one day I too would die. Someday my life on this earth would end. What then? I was filled with a mixture of horror, wonder, curiosity, regret, and acceptance of the inevitable.

This moment of truth comes to us all, but at different times. There are those like our son Stephen, who at the age of three, worried aloud about dying, perhaps because he was aware of the funerals his father had to conduct so often in church. On the other hand, there are those like my father who never really came to terms with dying until his death at the age of ninety-five. Whether this awareness of our own death comes early or late in life, we all have to face the fact that someday the bell will toll for us.

So, how do we, as Christians, handle the inevitability of our own death? Some look upon death as one of life's many stages. We are born, we live, and we die, and God is with us at every stage. Others look at death as a friend that rescues us from a severe illness or debilitating old age. Like St. Francis of Assisi, they welcome death as God's answer to human suffering. Still others see death as a promised transition to a new life with God. They agree with Victor Hugo, who wrote, "When I go down to the grave, I can say, like many others, 'I have finished my day's work.' But I cannot say, 'I have finished my life.' My day's work will begin the next morning. The tomb is not a blind alley; it is a thoroughfare. It closes on the twilight and opens on the dawn."

My husband comforted our son with the thought that Jesus assured us that God cares for us in life, so why should we doubt that God will continue to care for us in death? No matter how we look at the end of our life on earth, that is our comfort and our hope.

Prayer: *Death, where is your victory? Where is your sting? Thanks be to God, who gives us the victory through our Lord Jesus Christ! Amen.*

Adsum!

"For I am convinced that neither death, nor life, nor angels, nor rulers, nor things present, nor things to come, nor powers, nor height, nor depth, nor anything else in all creation, will be able to separate us from the love of God in Christ Jesus our Lord. (Romans 8:38-39)

When my husband died at the age of fifty-two, one of our seminary friends told me how difficult it was for him to call and talk with me. My husband was the first of his class to die, and his passing made him and his classmates suddenly all too aware of their own mortality. Another friend admitted he had wanted to comfort me, but hadn't known what to say. The thought of dying scared him to death, so it was easier not to talk about it. The leader of a grief workshop I attended commented that we have removed death so far from the home, and even the church, that some of today's seminary students have never attended a funeral, much less conducted one, until they get out into the parish.

No matter how much our contemporary culture denies death and avoids talking about it, we all have to face the fact that someday life as we know it on this earth will end. Someday the bell will toll for us, as it did for my husband and countless others, before and after him.

For Christians, death is simply one of life's many stages. For some of us, death may interrupt these stages and cut them short; for others, death may wait until we have lived through all of them. In the end, death comes to everyone. This is the way God has created us, and what God created is good. If death is a part of creation, then there must be goodness in death, and it need not be feared. The same God who is with us in birth and throughout our lives is with us at death. Jesus promised us that. God will be there waiting for us, ready to welcome us home.

In his fictional work *The Newcomes*, the Victorian novelist William M. Thackeray describes the death of old Colonel Newcome. Just before his passing, at the usual evening hour, the chapel bell of the school nearby began to toll. The old colonel's hands feebly beat time on the bed covers. Just as the last bell struck, a sweet smile lighted up his face. Lifting his head a little, he said "Adsum," and fell back. That was the Latin phrase for "I am present," which the boys had used when their names were called at school. The old colonel, his heart again that of a trusting child, had answered to his name as he stood in the presence of his Maker.

Prayer: *When the bell tolls for us, God, may we also answer "I am present," and come before you confident and unafraid, trusting that the promises of Jesus are true, and we will be welcomed home into your loving arms. Amen.*

What Will I Do?

I cry aloud to God, aloud to God, that he may hear me. In the day of my trouble I seek the Lord; in the night my hand is stretched out without wearying; my soul refuses to be comforted. (Psalm 77:1-2)

Losing a loved one is a terrible experience, no matter if it is a parent or spouse, a brother or sister, an infant or adult child. Whether the death is expected or unexpected, drawn out or sudden, we are never quite prepared for the awful, excruciating pain of separation that strikes deep within our being.

My husband died on an early Sunday morning in May, a bright and beautiful spring day. As I left the hospital to go home alone, I remember thinking, *how can the sun be shining today when my world has been shattered? Why isn't the sky dark with clouds, threatening the earth with thunder, lightning, and hail to match my desolate mood? What will I do without my beloved husband,* I thought; *how can I go on living when part of me is gone?*

The sun kept shining that day, the next day, and the day after that. The earth kept turning on its axis. Spring gave way to summer, summer to fall, fall to winter, and then it was spring again. I had survived a year, then another, and another. I went on without my husband, and I learned how to live with the pain of my loss. God, who knows only too well how it feels to lose a dear one, never left me alone in my misery. Through the concern and kindness of my family, friends, and neighbors, God comforted me with love and gave me hope that this new chapter of my life, though different, could be good.

Prayer:
When we lose a child or parent, husband dear, a wife, a friend,
there are painful empty places in our hearts until life's end.

Though we learn to go on living, no one takes a loved one's place.
Is this loneliness a curse, God, or a blessed gift of grace?

Look into these empty places at our hidden feelings, fears;
free us, God, from guilt and anger, and release love's healing tears.

Lead us to recall with laughter happy times with loved ones lost,
find the joy of loving others worth the pain that it has cost.

Let the love we shared together give us comfort, ease our pain,
that one day we may awaken to your rainbow in the rain.

Thank you, God, for empty places in our lives when loved ones die,
for they keep us still connected as the days and years pass by.[1]

---

1. *© Abingdon Press., 1998. Used by permission. All rights reserved. This hymn text is from* Time Now To Gather: New Hymns for the Church Family, *by Mary Nelson Keithahn and John Horman. (Abingdon Press, 1998).*

Embracing the Light

Coming to Terms with Being an Adult

When I was a child, I spoke like a child, I thought like a child, I reasoned like a child; when I became an adult, I put an end to childish ways. For now we see in a mirror, dimly, but then we will see face to face. Now I know only in part; then I will know fully.
(1 Corinthians 13:11-12)

When I moved from my home of twenty-two years, I spent weeks sorting through boxes in my storeroom and filling up dumpsters. Some of the boxes I unearthed contained memorabilia and journals from travels in this country and abroad. Each box brought back fond memories of people and places we had visited as a family, experiences that my children and I still treasured. Needless to say, most of these things went with me to my new home!

My husband loved to travel. Had he lived into retirement, I think he would have organized and led tours overseas, and we would have seen the world together. One of the first trips I made without him was to Germany and Austria in 1989 with our younger son, Stephen, who had a month between his last rotation and his June graduation from Duke Medical School. My German sister-in-law arranged for us to stay in the Frankfort and Munich areas with her relatives for part of our visit. After we arrived, they helped us plan an itinerary that took us by rented car to the Black Forest and through the Bavarian Alps to Innsbruck and Salzburg. As I re-read my journal from that time, I realized how precious that experience was, despite the fact that traveling without our husband and father was a painful reminder of his absence from our lives.

Three years earlier, when I was still in shock at my sudden and unexpected widowhood, I kept asking myself, "What will I do now?" Stephen had answered that question for me. "You are too young to live the rest of your life through your children. You will have to make a new life for yourself." I knew he was right, but it was hard to face being a widow with an empty nest, especially having grown up in a pre-feminist time. Taking responsibility for planning this trip with Stephen to celebrate his graduation was a big step for me. Though the experience was sometimes painful, because one we loved was absent, it helped us come to terms with our new relationship. We respected one another as adults now, but we were still mother and son. Our family did not die with our husband and father, and though Stephen and his siblings would no longer live in the same home or the same place with me, we would still share many good experiences in the years ahead.

Prayer: *How long it takes for us to become an adult in life, God, and even longer in our faith! Thank you for your patience and understanding as we struggle through that process. Amen.*

As A Father Has Compassion

As a father has compassion for his children, so the Lord has compassion for those who fear him. For he knows how we were made; he remembers that we are dust. As for mortals, their days are like grass; they flourish like a flower of the field; for the wind passes over it, and it is gone, and its place knows it no more. But the steadfast love of the Lord is from everlasting to everlasting on those who fear him, and his righteousness to children's children, to those who keep his covenant and remember to do his commandments. (Psalm 103:13-18)

A friend once shared with me the loneliness she had felt upon the death of her parents. Her immediate response to their loss had, of course, been shock and sorrow, and both physical and emotional pain. But the long-lasting effects of their deaths were the lonely feelings she experienced in being unable to talk things over with her parents, unable to share her joys and disappointments with them, unable to ask their advice or to do things for them.

The loneliness my "orphaned" friend experienced after the death of her parents is familiar to anyone who has lost a loved one. It has certainly been true in our family. My husband did not live to see our children marry, or get well-acquainted with their spouses. He missed out on the birth of our grandchildren, and subsequent baptisms, confirmations, and graduations. How often my children have wished that their father was still around to share in their lives! How often I have wished he was here to share our golden years of retirement!

That is why we have taken such comfort in the description of God found in Psalm 103, especially these words: *"As a father has compassion for his children, so the Lord has compassion for those who fear him....He knows how we were made....He remembers....He is steadfast in his love."* If the psalmist is right, and God does care for us like the best of human fathers, we are never alone in our loneliness. God is with us, sharing in our emptiness, listening to our needs, comforting us in our loneliness like a good father comforts his children.

Prayer: *We may be lonely, God, but we know we are never alone. You are always with us, holding us in your loving arms. Thank you. Amen.*

Be Not Afraid

Listen, I will tell you a mystery! We will not all die, but we will all be changed, in a moment, in the twinkling of an eye....[For] this mortal body must put on immortality....Then the saying that is written will be fulfilled: "Death has been swallowed up in victory."...Thanks be to God, who gives us the victory through our Lord Jesus Christ.
(1 Corinthians 15: 51-57, sel.)

When my junior high vacation church school class was studying worship, I asked each one in the class to develop a brief liturgy to share with the rest of the group. This involved identifying a subject, looking at it through the eyes of the Bible, and considering its meaning in their lives. The class members chose scriptures, wrote meditations and prayers, and selected appropriate hymns for their liturgies.

One girl's recent preoccupation with the mystery of death had aroused strong fears in her, and she decided to look at death from Paul's perspective in his first letter to the church at Corinth. After reflecting on chapter fifteen, she wrote this meditation:

> There are many types of fear. The one I am speaking of is the fear of death. At one time or another, you fear or will fear death. The letter Paul wrote to the Corinthians compared the human body now and the resurrected body to a seed this way: For an example, we will use a potato. You plant it in the ground and over a period of

weeks, roots spread out on the potato. Gradually the potato disintegrates and forms a plant, which is entirely different. Similarly, the body on earth is different from that of the resurrected body. This helps me because I know that when my body dies, life does not end. I will be with God. I cannot be separated from him.

About a month later, this girl's father was killed in a car accident. Death, for her, was no longer just a vague fear; it had become a reality to be faced. It was a time of inexpressible sorrow and anxiety about the future for her and her family, yet because she had already looked at death through the eyes of the Bible, she knew that life had not ended for her father; it had only changed. She knew also that God was grieving with her, and that she and her family and her father were all held fast in the everlasting arms of love.

Prayer: *How glad we are, God, that we can look at our fears and sorrows from the perspective of your Holy Word, and find comfort and hope in your love. Amen.*

Bear One Another's Burdens

Bear one another's burdens, and in this way you will fulfill the law of Christ. (Galatians 6:2)

Some years ago I received a Christmas card from a high school classmate I had not seen for a long time. In the card was a letter. "I wish I could sit down and talk with you," she wrote. "I'm so depressed and afraid. I've had two mastectomies this year, and my doctor says I'm terminal. My mother-in-law says my cancer is God's punishment for my sins. My mother says there is no God, so don't bother to pray."

What a burden my friend was carrying! When I visited my family in Minnesota the next week, I went to see her. I held her in my arms, and wept with her. I had lost my fifty-two-year-old husband five years earlier, and understood what lay ahead for her and her family. We talked together for a long time. I shared my faith that God does not cause illness and premature death; rather, God is with us when these tragic things happen, sharing in our suffering, weeping with us in our sorrow, comforting us with love and forgiveness, giving us the hope of eternal life.

I assured my friend of all these things, knowing in my heart that my words alone would have been ineffective if I had not come to be with her. God's loving presence is made known through our presence. Emmanuel, God with us, becomes real as we bear one another's burdens with love.

Prayer: *God, help us to take the time and make the effort to be with those who need us to share their burdens and assure them of your love. Amen.*

A Place for Me

Do not let your hearts be troubled. Believe in God, believe also in me. In my Father's house there are many dwelling places. If it were not so, would I have told you that I go to prepare a place for you? And if I go and prepare a place for you, I will come again and will take you to myself, so that where I am, there you may be also. (John 14:1-3)

People who live as long as I have are apt to attend a number of funerals and memorial services for friends and family members. Most likely they will hear this passage from the Gospel of John many times. Although the words are meant to be comforting and reassuring, they also cause us to wonder. Like children moving into a new home their parents have chosen, we ask, "What will our room in the new house be like?"

Whether we take this passage literally or metaphorically, death is life's last great mystery and we all wonder what comes next. What is this place that has been prepared for us? I think of it not as a physical place, but as a spiritual home filled with the warmth and light of God's presence. A home where God's loving spirit enables us to breathe and move easily, without pain. A home where we can put aside our fears and anxieties and focus on all that is beautiful and good. A home where the risen Christ is waiting to welcome us, along with our loved ones and friends who have arrived before us. A home where there is peace and rest.

I go to prepare a place for you.
I will come again and take you there.
I will be with you.

As a pastor, my husband had read this promise from Jesus many times at funerals he conducted before a heart attack ended his life prematurely. I think these words gave him the courage to face his own death unafraid, and they sustain me now as I await the day when I will find the answer to life's last great mystery for myself.

Prayer: *God, may we live out our days confident and unafraid, trusting that we will find a new home with you when our time on earth has ended. Amen.*

Salt of the Earth

You are the salt of the earth; but if salt has lost its taste, how can its saltiness be restored? It is no longer good for anything, but is thrown out and trampled under foot. (Matthew 5:13)

In Jesus' day, the salt that was readily available from the waters and shores of the Dead Sea was a valuable trade commodity. It was used to preserve and enhance the flavor of food, heal a toothache, and season sacrifices offered at the altar. Salt was so much a symbol of permanence and life for the Jews that they ate it to seal the covenants they made with one another. In fact, the presence of salt in every sacrifice may have reminded them of Yahweh's everlasting covenant with them.

Surprisingly, salt was also a symbol of death and destruction. Not only was the land around the Dead Sea barren and desolate, but armies often sowed conquered lands with salt to prevent any growth of crops.

Today our attitudes toward salt are still more ambiguous. We enjoy well-seasoned food, but the prevalence of hypertension and heart disease in our country has forced many of us to look for no-salt seasoning alternatives and avoid foods preserved with salt. We like to drive on safe winter highways, but the corrosive effects of salt on our automobiles has made it necessary to use other substances to prevent ice build-up on our roads.

If salt has so many negative side effects, then what do we do with Jesus' challenge to be the "salt of the earth"? Salt is pure. Salt is always noticeable; it makes a difference in the way food tastes. Salt keeps food from spoiling. As the "salt of the earth," we are called to be pure, to live according to Jesus' way of love. We are called to make a difference in the world by our loving presence and deeds, and to act in ways that will make it easier for other persons to be loving too. We are called to "flavor" their lives with the joy we have found in our faith. But always, we need to be careful of the side effects our actions may produce. We must listen, as well as speak; follow, as well as lead; learn, as well as teach; receive, as well as give.

Prayer: *Salt us with your goodness and love, God, that we may enrich and preserve your world for your glory. Amen.*

Mine or Ours?

The earth is the Lord's and all that is in it, the world, and those who live in it; for he has founded it on the seas, and established it on the rivers. (Psalm 24:1-2)

In one of his picture books, Leo Lionni told the story of three childlike frogs who spent each day quarreling in the pond where they lived.[1] "The water is mine," yelled Milton. "The earth is mine," claimed Rupert. "The air is mine," shouted Lydia. Finally a toad who lived on the other side of the island appeared to complain about the noise. "I can hear you shouting where I live," he told them. "This has to stop! No one will have any peace until you stop your bickering." But as soon as he left, the three little frogs began fighting again, this time over who owned the worm one had just found.

Then it began to rain, so heavily that the waters of the pond began to rise around the island where they lived. The frogs were scared. Even the stones they were sitting on began to disappear. Finally there was only one rock left. The three little frogs huddled there together, trembling with fear and cold, but feeling more secure because they were not alone. They were one in their hope the rain would soon stop, and it did. Imagine their surprise when they found the "rock" that had saved them was the back of the very toad that had complained about their bickering!

The little frogs had learned their lesson. From that day on, they swam together, chased butterflies together, and rested together in the weeds. "Isn't it peaceful," said Milton. "Isn't it beautiful," said Rupert. "And best of all," said Lydia, "it's ours!"

How different our world would be if everyone looked on its water, land, air, and living creatures as gifts from God, meant to be cared for and shared by all of God's children, instead of our own private property to use and exploit!

Prayer: *Creator God, help us remember that though the earth, and all that is in it, is ours to use, it still belongs to you, and you hold us accountable for the way we care for it and share its resources. May we all be more responsible stewards and friends to one another. Amen.*

1. It's Mine! *A fable by Leo Lionni (Alfred A. Knopf, 1985, 1986).*

Embracing the Light

A Mirror Image

Beloved, since God loved us so much, we also ought to love one another. No one has ever seen God; if we love one another, God lives in us, and his love is perfected in us. (1 John 4:11-12)

If someone asked you to draw a picture of God, what would you draw? A picture of Jesus, perhaps? After all, it is in Jesus that we see God's love most clearly: Jesus, the friend of those who have no friends; Jesus, the one who holds out his arms to children and welcomes them; Jesus, the teacher who shows us how to love one another; Jesus, the one who knows we all fall short of being the persons God created us to be and loves and forgives us still; Jesus, the one who suffers with us and for us; Jesus, the one who offers us hope and love.

As Christians, we are the Body of Christ in the world today, called to carry on this task of reflecting God's love to one another in our words and deeds. For example:

As a boy in India, my husband was aware of the many ways his missionary father was helping the poor farmers who lived in the villages and went out each day to work in fields that often belonged to other, wealthier families. His father showed the farmers how to dig wells to catch the monsoon rains to water their crops. He taught them how to fertilize and conserve the land. He convinced absentee landholders to give some of their lands to the people who farmed them. He started daycare programs for the young children whose parents worked in the fields. He assisted the villagers in building churches and starting health programs. In countless ways, my husband saw his father help the poor in the name of Christ. It didn't surprise him to hear a villager one day exclaim as his father walked by, "There goes God!"

The real challenge for us as Christians is this: What picture of God are we reflecting to one another in our lives? How are we helping one another see the God that was made known to us in Jesus Christ?

Prayer: *God, help us be mirror images of your love, reflecting your goodness and mercy in all we do and say. Amen.*

Trust God, Live for God

Do not keep striving for what you are to eat and what you are to drink, and do not keep worrying. For it is the nations of the world that strive after all these things, and your Father knows that you need them. Instead, strive for his kingdom, and these things will be given to you as well. (Luke 12:29-31)

Chico shivered in the cold mountain wind as he dug potatoes in a field on the Bolivian estate where he lived. He and his people were poor, little more than slaves of the patron who owned the land. As he dug, ever so often he would look around cautiously and slip a potato into his clothing. Later he would hide the potatoes in the field, and come back to find them when his hungry family needed a good meal. It was wrong, of course, but all the workers did it.

Then Benigno returned from the city. Benigno was the only one of Chico's people who was educated, and he had gone to the city to see about starting a school for them. He shook his head sadly when Chico asked what had happened. "A school is impossible," he said. "Our patron has friends in government. The education man told me if we started a school, he and I would both be arrested as revolutionaries and sent to prison!"

Benigno shared his disappointment with the community that night. Then he reminded them, "Jesus said to the poor around him, 'Seek first the kingdom of God, and all these things will be added to you.' I do not know how such a thing could be, but this is my word to you. Let us seek the kingdom of God and, if God wills, other things will be added to us."

Benigno began to teach everyone what he knew about living as Jesus had taught. First, they had to forgive their patron for the unjust way he had treated them, and second, they had to stop cheating him. It was hard, but Chico dug up his hidden potatoes for the foreman to find, and his brother, a shepherd, kept better watch of his sheep. Others did what they could. Though they wondered how they would survive the winter, they were content, trusting that God would care for them.

One day the patron called Benigno to appear before him. Everyone was afraid he would be punished, but the patron said, "I know how you have been teaching your people, and I also know that now they are fair and honest with me. Build your school and teach what you will."

Prayer: *Forgive us, God, when we become so preoccupied with our own needs that we forget how you want us to live. Help us instead to trust in your love enough to follow your way of love and justice, as hard as that may be. Amen.*

Embracing the Light

Lost and Found

When Jesus came to the place, he looked up and said to him, "Zacchaeus, hurry and come down; for I must stay at your house today."... All who saw it began to grumble and said, "He has gone to be the guest of one who is a sinner." Zacchaeus stood there and said to the Lord, "Look, half of my possessions, Lord, I will give to the poor; and if I have defrauded anyone of anything, I will pay back four times as much." Then Jesus said to him, "Today salvation has come to this house...for the Son of Man came to seek out and to save the lost."
(Luke 19:5-10, sel.)

Getting lost is a frightening experience, especially when you are in a strange country and cannot read or speak the language. On the night our family of six arrived in Kyoto, Japan, we had to take two cabs from the train station to our inn. The first cab driver did not speak English, but seemed to recognize the address a missionary had written in Japanese characters on a post card. The three younger children and I went with him, while my husband and older son waited to bring our luggage in a second cab.

What we did not realize until later was that specific addresses in Kyoto were hard for even cab drivers to find! The streets were narrow and crowded, and the houses were numbered in the order in which they were built, not according to their location. The cab driver let us out in the general area, but as soon as he left, we realized we were lost. There was nothing that looked like an inn on this street! To make matters worst, my husband had kept the only card we had with its name and address!

All we could do was go up to the nearest house and ask for help. Somehow, mostly through sign language, we managed to communicate our plight to the kind family who opened the door. They invited us inside, gave snacks to the children, and served us tea in their tatami room, while the father tried to help us find our inn. The missionary who had arranged our lodging taught at Doshisha University, a well-known Christian institution. Our host contacted the missionary's wife there, got the name of the inn, and called the innkeeper to explain what had happened. Much to our relief, my husband and older son soon came to get us.

That experience of being lost and found, and being cared for so graciously by strangers, gave us a new perspective on the way love works. On our flight back home we noticed a young man from Japan traveling alone, and realized how confusing things would be to him in our country and how lost he might feel. We made a point of getting acquainted with him, and he was happy to accept our invitation to spend a few days with us in our home before reporting for college.

Prayer: *God, like Zacchaeus, we have known the loneliness of being lost and the joy of being found, and we have been forever changed by this experience. May we, like that tax collector, find ways to pass on the compassion and kindness we have received to others in Christ's name. Amen.*

Embracing the Light

Second Thoughts

But God has so arranged the body...that...the members may have the same care for one another. If one member suffers, all suffer together with it. (1 Corinthians 12:24b-26, sel.)

Almost every morning, I wake up to the daily news on National Public Radio. For many years I enjoyed Garrison Keillor's brief segment, *The Writer's Almanac.* One day he reminded us that it was the anniversary of the Titanic's setting sail on her ill-fated maiden voyage across the North Atlantic. Then he sang a few lines from a little ditty about that tragedy. Like Garrison Keillor, I grew up in Minnesota, and I think we sang many of the same songs for fun. I hadn't thought of this one in years, but the words immediately came back to me, and I found I could still sing the whole thing to its lively tune:

> Oh, they built the ship Titanic to sail the ocean blue,
> and they thought they had a ship that the water could
> ne'er go through.
> It was on her maiden trip when the iceberg hit the ship.
> It was sad when the great ship went down.
> Oh, it was sad (it was sad),
> It was sad (it was sad),
> It was sad when the great ship went down
> to the bottom of the sea (Husbands and wives,
> little-bitty children lost their lives)
> It was sad when the great ship went down.

Then it hit me. This was one of the "fun" songs we had sung in our church youth groups and camps. How could we have sung about this terrible event in such a light-hearted manner! What were we thinking? In our young pre-electronics world, the tragic loss of all those people was an event that happened long ago and far away. It did not touch us personally. The song was just another song among many. I wish someone had read us this poem by John Donne:

> No man is an island,
> Entire of itself.
> Every man is a piece of the continent,
> A part of the main.
> If a clod be washed away by the sea,
> Europe is the less.
> As well as if a promontory were.
> As well as if a manor of thy friend's
> Or of thine own were:
> Any man's death diminishes me,
> Because I am involved in mankind,
> And therefore never send to know for whom the bell tolls;
> It tolls for thee.[1]

Prayer: *Forgive us, God, when we are insensitive to the suffering of others, and remind us that you call us to bear one another's burdens as if they were our own. Amen.*

---

1. *Excerpt from* Meditation XVII in Devotions Upon Emergent Occasions, *by John Donne, 1624 (CreateSpace Independent Publishing Platform, 2013).*

I Have Fought the Good Fight

I have fought the good fight, I have finished the race, I have kept the faith. From now on there is reserved for me the crown of righteousness. (2 Timothy 4:7-8a)

Paul wrote these words in a letter to his young coworker Timothy when he was nearing the end of his ministry. In reflecting on the way he had answered God's call, he compared his life to an athlete competing for the victor's wreath of laurel, the prize in athletic contests of his day.

"The good fight" probably was a reference to the ancient sport of Greco-Roman wrestling that is still a part of the Summer Olympics today. It is an appropriate analogy for the Christian life. Our sons and a grandson were all wrestlers, and I spent many hours watching them and their teammates compete. I know the discipline and training involved in that sport; the importance of having a keen mind, self-confidence, and enthusiasm for its challenges; the need to be committed to putting forth your best efforts and accepting responsibilities for the results, win or lose. I know too that although each wrestling match is a separate event, it is also part of a team effort, and encouragement to and from teammates is important. These are the kind of qualities that help us wrestle with our calling as members of the Christian community.

In the ancient games, Paul would have watched foot-races as well as wrestling matches, and he saw "finishing the course" as another metaphor for the Christian life. Our younger daughter was a runner, and we often watched her compete. I learned that how you start a race is important, but it is often how you finish it that makes the difference in where you place. Medals are won by that extra kick, a final burst of speed on the last stretch, and a determination to cross the finish line despite your pain. I also saw how important it is to have family and friends cheer you on, comfort you when you lose, and rejoice with you when you win. So it is with the Christian life. We have little control over how long we have to race through life, but God expects us to do our best and finish the course.

"I have kept the faith," Paul wrote. God had entrusted him with the gift of faith. He had cherished it and used it well. Now it was time to hand it on to others, and with it, the task of ministering to the young churches he had gathered. It was time for Paul to rest on his laurels.

Prayer: *God, whether we are at the beginning or the end of our life as Christians, may we always be able to say, "we have fought the good fight, we have finished the race, we have kept the faith." Amen.*

The Ripple Effect

We do not live to ourselves, and we do not die to ourselves.…Let us therefore…resolve instead never to put a stumbling block or hindrance in the way of another. I know and am persuaded in the Lord Jesus that nothing is unclean in itself; but it is unclean for anyone who thinks it unclean. If your brother or sister is being injured by what you eat, you are no longer walking in love. Do not let what you eat cause the ruin of one for whom Christ died. (Romans 14:7, 13b-15)

One of my favorite contemporary humorists is Garrison Keillor, perhaps because I too grew up in Minnesota and feel I know all the characters in his Lake Wobegon stories personally. Perhaps it's because I have been struck by the religious insights in his work. Keillor's stories help us look at ourselves and our neighbors through the eyes of faith, chuckling with God over our foolish ways, weeping tears of sorrow in our tragedies and tears of happiness in our triumphs, and trusting that God has more joyful surprises ahead for us.

Take, for example, Keillor's story, "Letter from Jim,"[1] about a man who contemplates adultery with a colleague until he begins to think about the ripple effect of his moral (or immoral) choices on others. Jim is going through a mid-life crisis. When he loses his long-time job as a teacher in the classics department at the age of forty and his family doesn't want to move, he takes a job in the college admissions office that is twice the work at one-fourth less pay. His wife is unsympathetic, his children expect him to continue supporting them in the style to which they are accustomed, and his oldest can now beat him in a pick-up game of basketball! He feels old and unappreciated.

Jim's coworker is a beautiful young woman who is lonely in the little college town. Jim advises her to make friends, and she makes friends with him. She makes him feel funny and smart and handsome. They decide to attend a conference in Chicago together, and she offers to drive. Jim doesn't know what she had in mind, but he has adultery in his heart. However, after he packs his bag, says goodbye to his family, kisses his wife, and is sitting in the yard, waiting for his ride, he starts thinking. *Adultery is simple*, he says to himself. He looks down the street and thinks about all the decent, ordinary people who are his neighbors, and how much they depend on one another. He thinks about how his infidelity would hurt them if it became known, as he knows it would. *If I go to Chicago with a woman that is not my wife*, he says to himself, *the school patrol will forget to guard the crossing, a teacher without a thought will eliminate South America from geography, our minister will toss out his sermon on the poor, and the butcher will decide yesterday's sausage is good enough for today. No one will care about doing what is right.* His letter ends, "We depend on one another more than we know." And somehow we know he will not risk hurting his family or friends.

Prayer: *God, whenever we are tempted to make a wrong choice, help us think about how our actions might hurt others, and choose the way of love. Amen.*

---

1. *Adapted from an excerpt from a live broadcast of A Prairie Home Companion on American Public Radio, and recorded with other stories on a set of four cassette tapes entitled* News *from Lake Wobegon. © 1983, Minnesota Public Radio.*

Embracing the Light

The Least of These

*Truly I tell you, just as you did it to one of the least of these who are
members of my family, you did it to me.....As you did not do it to one of
the least of these, you did not do it to me.* (Matthew 25:40, 45)

For several years I served as a Court Appointed Special Advocate
(CASA) for children who end up in the court system as a result of
parental neglect or abuse. This experience made me aware of the
many families in our area who go through life virtually untouched
by any church. They are often people with alcohol or drug problems
or histories of abuse going back several generations. They have never
learned good social or parenting skills because they have grown up
in homes without them. Sometimes they have physical or mental
disabilities, and lack organizational and management skills. They
suffer from poor nutrition and personal hygiene. Their friends are
often in similar circumstances.

One of my CASA families had tried out different congregations, but
had never found a church home. I could not help but wonder how
this family had been treated when they appeared for worship. Had
they found a welcome, or had the members of that congregation
seen their overwhelming needs and looked away?

Of course, well-to-do, professional, educated, productive persons
are more attractive prospects for church membership. We would
all rather add more resources to our congregation than expend
what we have on the poor. But if we are really going to follow

Jesus' example and carry on his work, how can we avoid opening our doors and our hearts to the "least of these?" What the families I encountered needed most were positive peer relationships, and a caring community of friends with the patience to help them learn basic social skills and grow in their roles as parents. They needed a congregation that would help them discover that God loves and cares for them too. If we could offer them this kind of support, what a difference we could make in their lives!

Prayer: *God of the open arms, give us the courage and compassion we need to reach out and surround the "least of your children" with love, and welcome them into our midst. Amen.*

Competitors or Colleagues?

John answered, "Master, we saw someone casting out demons in your name, and we tried to stop him, because he does not follow with us." But Jesus said to him, "Do not stop him; for whoever is not against you is for you." (Luke 9:49-50)

In our polarized world of the twenty-first century, the gulf between political parties, economic and social classes, and even faith communities seems to be growing wider and wider. We all seem bent on preventing the "others" from usurping our power and place in life, and there is little appetite for appreciating the contributions of rivals, or an honest discussion of differences, or working together for the common good. Sadly, this is especially true in the area of religion. Like the disciples of Jesus in this incident from the Gospel of Luke, we each want to preserve our identity and mission for ourselves.

This is not a new problem. When I was growing up in a small town in Minnesota, the climate among the churches in the community was one of competition, rather than cooperation, and suspicion, rather than trust. School board elections were decided along denominational lines. Catholics wouldn't vote for Lutherans and Lutherans wouldn't vote for Catholics, so they gave their votes to the Congregational candidates. An informal quota system for hiring new public school teachers made sure their religious preferences would reflect the make-up of the community. Only a few churches participated in then-legal high school baccalaureate services, and ecumenical services were nonexistent. Families socialized mainly with other families in their congregations. Denominational loyalties were also ethnic: Irish Catholics, English Congregationalists, German Lutherans, Norwegian or Swedish Lutherans.

By the time we were serving a church in another small Minnesota town in the mid-1960s, attitudes had changed. We participated in ecumenical teacher-training opportunities, curriculum development, and choral directors' groups, and worshipped with other congregations several times a year. We were colleagues, appreciating and encouraging one another in our different approaches to a common mission.

Eighteen years later we moved to the Black Hills where we found the pendulum swinging back in time. As denominational identity became less important to people, churches became more protective of their "territory." Denominations clashed over social issues, doctrinal positions, music and worship styles, and approaches to youth ministry. Once more we saw one another as competitors, not colleagues. It seems we would all do well to read Jesus' words to his disciples again!

Prayer: *God, help us to respect our neighbors and bridge the gulfs that lie between us. Amen.*

Whatever You Do

As God's chosen ones, holy and beloved, clothe yourselves with compassion, kindness, humility, meekness, and patience. Bear with one another and, if anyone has a complaint against another, forgive each other; just as the Lord has forgiven you, so you must also forgive. Above all, clothe yourselves with love, which binds everything together in perfect harmony.... And whatever you do, in word or deed, do everything in the name of the Lord Jesus, giving thanks to God the Father through him. (Colossians 3:12-14, 17)

On our visit to Japan in 1972, missionary friends told us about the Kobayashi family. Mrs. Kobayashi's father had had no sons to carry on the family name, so when she married, her husband took her family name as his own. A man who did this was called an "omuko-san" and treated as little more than a servant. Mr. Kobayashi was not satisfied with this traditional role, and became a leader among other young men in their village. He helped organize a volunteer fire department and once, when a flood came, almost lost his life as the firemen worked to save the riverbanks. This experience led him to the Christian church where he felt Christ's call to be baptized.

Mrs. Kobayashi's father, livid with anger, denounced his son-in-law in a drunken rage, and Mr. Kobayashi left home, intending never to return. The Christian pastor encouraged him to try again, and he went back. His father-in-law, a farmer, had squandered the family money and property, so Mr. Kobayashi had to find a job to support the family. At first he was afraid to admit he was a Christian on the application, lest he wouldn't get the job, but then he decided not to hide his new faith. The official who interviewed him told him that the agricultural cooperative needed men with his spirit, and hired him.

Mr. Kobyashi rewarded the official's trust in him with loyalty and hard work. His wife and her family grudgingly came to recognize his faith as a positive force in his life. The Kobayashis sent their four sons to the local church-related kindergarten and to Sunday School, and after many years, Mrs. Kobyashi finally declared her faith and was baptized too.

Prayer: *Gift us with your spirit, God, that we too may be faithful in all things, compassionate and kind to one another, forgiving of those who hurt us, and patient in waiting for your love to take hold in their lives. Amen.*

A Quiet Place

The apostles gathered around Jesus, and told him all that they had done and taught. He said to them, "Come away to a deserted place all by yourselves and rest a while." For many were coming and going, and they had no leisure even to eat. And they went away in the boat to a deserted place by themselves. (Mark 6:30-32)

It is said that the island of Iona on the west coast of Scotland is one of those "thin" places where the physical and spiritual worlds come together, and people feel most strongly connected with the presence of God. My daughter and I can attest to that. In the summer of 2005, we joined a small group from the Black Hills of South Dakota on a pilgrimage to Iona. Four years earlier, Becky's husband had died after a long illness. She was ready now to make some decisions about her future, and needed time away from her busy life as a parent and teacher to think and pray. I had been longing to visit the Iona Community and experience it for myself.

As soon as we arrived on Iona, it was apparent that our week on this tiny island would be different from any other we had experienced. For one thing, we were housed in the restored thirteenth-century Benedictine abbey. (A bonus for a mystery fan like me who has read all the Brother Cadfael and Sister Fidelma mysteries. Fortunately, no bodies surfaced that week!) Leaders of the Community emphasized that this was not a workshop that would provide us with new skills, or a retreat where we would spend much of our time in silence. Rather, it was an experience in living in Christian community. We would worship, work, eat, study the Bible, play, and go on pilgrimages together. Daily agendas would be posted, but we were free to choose what we wanted to do. It was an adjustment for Type A personalities like us, but we relaxed and entered into the experience whole-heartedly. Surprisingly, within the rhythm of life in the Iona Community, we found time for long, quiet walks alone or with new friends, time for mutual sharing and reflection, and time for feeling God's presence, not just in the wild beauty of the island, but in this caring community. Becky and I came home refreshed and renewed, with a new sense of purpose in our lives.

We can't all go to Iona, but we can be intentional about finding a quiet time and place to connect with God's presence and discover God's plan for our lives.

> *Come away with me to a quiet place,*
> *apart from the world with its frantic pace,*
> *to pray, reflect, and seek God's grace,*
> *Come away with me. Come away.*[1]

Prayer: *Call us away from the world into your quiet presence, God, and speak to us the words we need. Amen.*

---

1. © *Abingdon Press, 1998. Used by permission. All rights reserved. First stanza of a hymn included in* Come Away With Me: A Collection of Original Hymns *by Mary Nelson Keithahn and John D. Horman. (Abingdon Press, 1998). The hymn is also in the supplements* The Faith We Sing *(Abingdon Press, 2000),* Sing The Faith *(Geneva Press, 2003), and* Upper Room Worshipbook: Music and Liturgies for Spiritual Formation *(Upper Room Books, 2006).*

Embracing the Light

A Better Way

All who exalt themselves will be humbled, but all who humble themselves will be exalted. (Luke 18:14b)

Among the folktales collected by the Brothers Grimm was the story of "The Fisherman and His Wife."[1] It is about a couple that lived in a tiny hut near the sea. One day the fisherman hooked a great fish, and with much effort, landed it. To his surprise, the fish cried out, "I am not a fish at all. I am an enchanted prince. Please throw me back into the water and let me live." The fisherman was a kindly man, and did as he was asked.

When he went home and told his wife about the fish, she was very angry. "You mean you let the prince go without asking anything in return?" she shouted. "Go back and ask that fish for a better house." Reluctantly the fisherman returned to the shore and called:

> *Oh, magical fish, oh, fish in the sea,*
> *Pray, grant the wish that my wife begs of thee.*

The fish appeared, and the fisherman repeated his wife's request. The fish said, "Go home, she has her house." But when the fisherman went home, he found his wife was still not satisfied. She sent him back to the fish again and again, first for a mansion, then for a castle. Then she wanted to be king, the emperor, and finally the pope! Each time the fish granted her request. But when she asked to be God, the fish said to the fisherman, "Go home, your wife is sitting in your hut."

God is good. God gives us all that we need, and often much of what we want as well. But when we are tempted to give ourselves god-like powers and try to control the lives of others for our own benefit, God says "No!" This is not the way of Jesus, who:

> *though he was in the form of God, did not regard equality with God as something to be exploited, but emptied himself, taking the form of a slave, being born in human likeness. And being found in human form, he humbled himself and became obedient to the point of death—even death on a cross.*
> (Philippians 2:6-8)

Prayer: *Forgive us, God, for our discontent and our willingness to use any means to get what we want. Help us to choose a better way, the way of love, the Way of Jesus Christ. Amen.*

1. *One of the picture book versions of this story is* The Fisherman and His Wife, *by Margot Zemach (W.W. Norton & Company, Inc., 1966).*

Big and Little

[Jesus told a] parable to some who trusted in themselves that they were
righteous and regarded others with contempt. (Luke 18:9)

In her picture book version of an old fable from India,[1] Marcia
Brown tells about a hermit who lived alone, spending most of his
time in meditation. One day, when he was thinking about "big"
and "little," he saw a mouse about to be snatched up by a crow.
He rescued the mouse, and took him back to his hut in the forest,
where he fed and comforted him. But then a cat came to the hut,
and the hermit was afraid for his pet. Since he knew magic as well
as prayer, he quickly changed the mouse into a bigger cat that could
hold his own against the intruder. That night, when a dog barked
in the forest the cat hid under his bed, so the hermit changed him
into an even bigger, stronger dog. Not long after that, a hungry
tiger came looking for food and attacked the dog. Fortunately, the
hermit was near-by, and with a wave of his hand, the dog was a
handsome, royal tiger.

Now this tiger was very proud of himself, and all day long paraded
around the forest, lording it over the other animals. The hermit
was disappointed in him. "Without me," he said, "you would be
a wretched little mouse; that is, if you were still alive. There is no
need to put on such airs."

The tiger was angry and hurt. He forgot all that the hermit had
done for him. "No one will tell me that I was once a mouse," he
roared. "I will kill him!"

But the hermit read the tiger's mind. "Go back to the forest, you ungrateful creature, and be a mouse again!" The tiger vanished, and a frightened, humble little mouse ran off into the forest. The hermit sat quietly, thinking again about "big" and "little."

Prayer: *Forgive us, God, when we act like the little mouse in this*
          fable, and forget that you are the source of all that is
          good in us. Forgive us when we misuse the freedom you have
          given us to serve our selfish needs. Give us instead big hearts,
          filled with gratitude for your good gifts and the desire to share
          these gifts with others. Amen.

1. Once A Mouse, *by Marcia Brown (Charles Scribner's Sons, 1961).*

Embracing the Light

Light in the Darkness

My God, my God, why have you forsaken me? Why are you so far from helping me, from the words of my groaning? (Psalm 22:1)

Martin Luther had tried hard to be a faithful priest, but he couldn't get past the feeling that he could never be good enough to satisfy God. He followed everything the Church prescribed, but nothing helped. He was the same man with the same weaknesses and problems as before. Finally, he turned to the Bible and found an answer in Paul's letter to the church at Rome. In Jesus Christ, God became one of us, suffered with us, forgave us, and accepted us as if we had done no wrong. All we have to do is repent of our wrongs and trust in God's love.

Martin was so excited about this good news that he began telling others about it. He hadn't meant to start a new movement, but people listened, and began following his way of thinking. This made the Church leaders angry, and he was forced to leave his monastery. He kept on teaching and preaching, and married a former nun whose name was Katie. After he publicly challenged some of the Church's beliefs he was severely criticized and in constant danger from his enemies.

Martin frequently became so discouraged and depressed by this situation that he would sit for hours, unable to work. On one of these occasions, Katie Luther entered the room and pulled all the shades on the windows. Then she draped the room in black, as if for a funeral. When her husband asked her who had died, she replied, "Why, from the way you have been acting, I thought God must have died!" Shaken from his black mood, Martin laughed and went back to work.

How often we let ourselves live as if God were dead! We despair when our actions have unintended consequences, our plans fail, our dreams fade, our hopes go unfilled. We forget that the God who came to us in Jesus still lives and acts in our lives. God still has a plan for us, no matter how blind we are to its purpose. We are never forsaken. We are always in God's care.

Prayer: *Living and loving God, help us to trust in your will for our lives, and give us the faith we need to face the challenges of each new day with joy and hope. Amen.*

No One Has Greater Love

This is my commandment, that you love one another as I have loved you. No one has greater love than this, to lay down one's life for one's friends. (John 15:12-13)

Alban lived in a little town in fourth-century England. Rich and talented, he had everything any young Roman could desire. He also had a kind and generous heart, and his door was always open to anyone who needed help. One day, a Christian priest came to him, asking for a place to hide. "The soldiers are searching for me," he said. It was a crime to be a Christian now, and many Christians were treated badly by the Romans. Alban was amazed at their courage, and had wanted to learn more about their faith for some time. He gave the old priest shelter, and made up his mind to find out all he could about his faith.

As Alban and the priest sat talking night after night, Alban became more impressed. He noticed that the old man spent a lot of time talking to someone he could not see. "I'm praying to my God," the old man told him. "Although we cannot see him, we Christians know that God is always with us. That is why we are never lonely or afraid."

This was their secret then, Alban thought. Their God was a living force in their lives, giving them courage to face whatever happened to them. He was not a lifeless statue of some imagined god, or a Roman emperor whom no one respected. That night Alban prayed his first prayer to the God of the Christians, and he realized that he too now shared their faith.

Eventually the soldiers heard where the old priest was hiding and came for him. When they entered the house, Alban was standing to greet them, wearing the old man's robes. It was not until they brought him before their officer that they realized their mistake. "You have brought me the wrong man!" shouted the officer. But Alban told him calmly, "I am a Christian now too. You have the right man after all." The officer tried to persuade him to change his mind, but Alban kept his faith and courageously went to his death.[1]

Prayer: *We do not ask you to make our lives easier, God. We pray only for courage to face the hard tasks and decisions ahead of us, and faith to let our love for you and one another guide our actions. Amen.*

1. *This story was adapted from "Saint Alban and the Priest," a story that was included in* Stories for School Prayers, *by Eileen Scott (London: National Society S.P.C.K., 1962).*

Embracing the Light

A Time to Remember

You shall not take vengeance or bear a grudge against any of your people, but you shall love your neighbor as yourself: I am the Lord... When an alien resides with you in your land, you shall not oppress the alien. The alien who resides with you shall be to you as the citizen among you; you shall love the alien as yourself, for you were aliens in the land of Egypt: I am the Lord your God. (Leviticus 19:18, 33-34)

My paternal grandparents emigrated from Sweden to Minnesota in the last part of the nineteenth century. I have found they had one thing in common: They were poor and they had worked very hard from an early age. That was not surprising, for Sweden was one of the poorest countries in Europe, and almost everyone was poor. What saved them was that the rich were not so rich as the richest nobles in the other countries, the poor were not so poor as the poorest, and there was a large middle class of farmers represented in their government. These farmers knew the plight of the poor, for they had often been the "crofters" allowed to build simple houses on small plots of land on their farms in exchange for their labor. They saw to it that Sweden developed a system for caring for the poorest among them: the sick, the old, widows, single mothers, and orphans. There were community "poor houses" where everyone lived in one big room with few comforts and plain food, but no one was without shelter. Sometimes poor families were rotated around better-off families who took them in for a month and then sent them on to someone else. Being homeless was not an option. Anyone who moved from one place to another had to have a "moving in, moving out" certificate as proof that they had a job or some means of support waiting for them.

The Swedes figured out a way to care for their neighbors, because even those who improved their status never forgot what it meant to be poor, and they knew that they might be the next ones to need help. When people emigrated from Sweden to this country, they brought their concern for a social support system for the poor with them, and their influence has been evident over the years in a state like Minnesota, and in agencies like Lutheran Social Services.

My mother's ancestors arrived on the Mayflower in Massachusetts in 1620 and a century later in the Middle Atlantic states with William Penn's fleet of ships from Northern Ireland. They were all immigrants too, with their own needs and special gifts to offer. They were once "aliens" in this land, just like almost everyone else in this country. We need to remember that in current discussions about our immigration policies. Perhaps we should all read these words from Leviticus again!

Prayer: *God, whose love is all-inclusive, may we welcome the immigrants among us, and offer them the refuge, hope, and chance for a new life that our ancestors received when they arrived in this land. Amen.*

They're Only Children

An argument arose among them as to which one of them was the greatest. But Jesus, aware of their inner thoughts, took a little child and put it by his side, and said to them, "Whoever welcomes this child in my name welcomes me, and whoever welcomes me welcomes the one who sent me; for the least among all of you is the greatest." (Luke 9:46-48)

In mainline congregations like ours, people often bemoan the fact that we don't have more children involved in our church school and other activities. They see children as the future of the church, and when they are scarce, the future looks dismal indeed! Yet these same congregations often downgrade those who work with children in comments like these: "It's only a children's choir. You can direct it." "I don't know how to teach adults, but I'll try taking the kindergarten class. They're only children, and I surely will know as much as they do about God." "Let's ask a layperson to do the children's times in worship this month. There's not much preparation required. After all, they're only children!"

For most of my life, I have felt called to a holistic ministry to children and youth through education, worship, and music. In volunteer and paid positions, I have served as a church educator, taught classes, directed choirs, organized and led music, art, and drama camps, developed curriculum resources, written numerous articles for a variety of journals and several books, and led workshops at regional and national events. Yet, like almost everyone else who works with children in the church, I have been frustrated by the way our ministries are considered less important because, after all, we only work with children.

Attitudes like these imply that the needs and abilities of children are secondary to those of adults, that children do not deserve well-trained, capable teachers, and that only those who lack the skills to work with adults should be assigned to teach the children. Perhaps one of the reasons there are fewer children in our congregations today is that these attitudes influence how we plan for and support our ministry to "the least of these" among us.

Jesus displayed a different attitude when he responded to the argument his disciples were having over who was the greatest. He affirmed the value of the child he called to sit beside him, and told his friends that welcoming children and serving their needs was the greatest work of all.

Prayer: *They're only children, God, but Jesus has helped us see them through your eyes as worthy of the best we have to offer them. Amen.*

The Ultimate Gift

"If any want to become my followers, let them deny themselves and take up their cross and follow me. For those who want to save their life will lose it, and those who lose their life for my sake, and for the sake of the gospel, will save it." (Mark 8:34-35)

In 1984, my husband, son Philip, and I went to South India to visit my father-in-law who was nearing the end of a long life of service working in the villages there. On our way home we stopped to see our seminary classmates (and my son's godparents) at Ahmednagar College, in the city of Ahmednagar, east of Mumbai and Poona.

When we returned home, I was intrigued to note that a hymn we had used in church school had its origins in Ahmednagar. The hymn was written in the Marathi language by Krishnarao Sangle in the nineteenth century, and later translated into English. Sangle was a Hindu who became a Christian as a result of his experiences in our Congregational mission schools. His parents and elder brother strongly opposed his decision to be baptized. In those days, this probably meant his family would have nothing more to do with him. He literally gave up everything when he became a Christian.

The hymn he wrote came straight from his heart:

> *Heart and mind, possessions Lord,*
> *I offer unto thee;*
> *all these were thine, Lord;*
> *thou didst give them unto me.*
> *Wondrous are thy doings unto me.*
> *Plans and my thoughts and everything I do*
> *are dependent on thy will and love alone.*
> *I commit my spirit unto thee.*[1]

When I am tempted to say, "No, I can't give any more of my time or my resources or myself to God's work," I think of Krishnarao Sangle who gave his all, and I am ashamed of my reluctance to be more sacrificial in my giving.

Prayer: *You gave us life, God, and new life in Christ. May we be*
          as willing to give of ourselves to you. Amen.

---

1. *This is the first stanza of the hymn written by Krishnarao Rathnaji Sangle (1834–1908), translated by Alden H. Clark (1878), and incuded with the Marathi tune, TNANA MANA DHANA, in the* Pilgrim Hymnal *(The Pilgrim Press, 1958).*

Happiness Is...

Happy are those whose help is the God of Jacob, whose hope is in the Lord their God, who made heaven and earth, the sea, and all that is in them; who keeps faith forever; who executes justice for the oppressed; who gives food to the hungry. (Psalm 146:5-7)

Happy are those who are kind to the poor (Proverbs 14:21b)...*who trust in the Lord* (Proverbs 16:20)...*who keep [God's] ways* (Proverbs 8:32b)...*who find wisdom and understanding.* (Proverbs 3:13)

Our family has always enjoyed Broadway musicals. One of our favorites is *You're a Good Man, Charlie Brown.*[1] We saw it in an off-Broadway theater when we were in New York in 1970, and our two older children later played Schroeder and Lucy in their high school production. After we moved to South Dakota we saw the musical performed at the Black Hills Playhouse. One of the songs, "Happiness," has always given me reason to reflect. What is it that really makes us happy? What is it that brings us joy?

One Sunday I explored these questions with children during their time in worship. First, we talked about the different ways they were measured: their height, their weight, how fast they could run, how high they could jump. Then I got out a tape measure and measured their smiles! Of course, they all put on their happiest faces. When I asked the children what made them smile, they came up with a variety of answers: A funny story, a new puppy, chocolate chip cookies, a hug from Grandpa, doing better on a spelling test, making up with a friend after a fight, being forgiven for dropping the eggs.

We're all happy for different reasons, I concluded, but there is a special kind of happiness that comes from following Jesus. This poem I learned as a child for our Sunday School Christmas program tells it all:

> Happiness is…
> showing love to your family and friends;
> helping cheerfully at home;
> being a friend to lonely people;
> feeding children who are hungry;
> being kind to everyone, even those we don't like;
> bringing joy to others;
> for this is how we celebrate the life of Jesus.
> Happiness comes to everyone who follows in his
> way of love.

Prayer: *God, thank you for showing us what true happiness is. May we always find our joy in following Jesus. Amen.*

---

1. *A 1967 musical comedy with music and lyrics by Clark Gesner, based on characters from the syndicated Peanuts comicstrip created by Charles Schultz.*

Embracing the Light

Good for Nothing

But love your enemies, do good, and lend, expecting nothing in return.
(Luke 6:35a)

In an old cartoon, Blondie and Elmo, the helpful little neighbor boy, have just brought armloads of groceries into the Bumstead kitchen. Blondie attempts to pay Elmo for his help, but he refuses her offer, saying, "December is when kids are good for nothing!" As he leaves, Blondie says, "That didn't sound right, but it does make sense!"

Good for nothing! How often we have heard that term used in a derogatory way: That good-for-nothing dog has just tracked mud all over my kitchen floor again! That good-for-nothing husband of hers can't even support his family! That good-for-nothing girl just smashed up her car for the second time! But Elmo did not have someone's thoughtlessness, or financial failures, or carelessness in mind. Elmo was talking about being good without expecting anything in return.

We can all remember people who have been good to us for nothing: parents who sacrificed to give us opportunities they had not had; a teacher who took the time to give us extra help and encouragement; a neighbor who left his own fields to help with the harvest when we were ill; a friend who put aside a busy schedule to listen to our troubles; a banker who helped us resolve our financial problems; a minister who came when we needed pastoral care. They were all there for us, asking nothing in return, evidence of the amazing grace that comes ultimately from God.

In the presence of such unselfish love, we are haunted by the times we have failed to be good for nothing, when we were helpful only because we expected something in return. We remember, and are ashamed.

Prayer: *Forgive us, God, when we forget that your love does not let us rest until we pass it on. Make us aware of all those in need of a loving friend. Help us to be good to them, good for nothing. Amen.*

The Miserables

And [Jesus] answered them, "Go and tell John what you have seen and heard: the blind receive their sight, the lame walk, the lepers are cleansed, the deaf hear, the dead are raised, the poor have good news brought to them." (Luke 7:22)

My granddaughter Katie and I were part of a group that toured the Hashemite Kingdom of Jordan in 2005. When we were in Aqaba, we kept returning to an art gallery near our hotel. The gallery was owned and operated by the artist whose pictures were on display. She had been a high school art teacher, and Katie enjoyed visiting with her.

After much deliberation, Katie chose a realistic painting of a desert scene, with Bedouins, tents, and camels. I intended to buy something similar as a reminder of our time in Wadi Rum, but I found myself drawn to a painting the artist had done in a more abstract style. The painting was a head and shoulders portrait of three persons, generic as to gender, ethnicity, and class, against a dark blue background. The heads are inclined slightly to their right, and their sad eyes seemed to look deep into my heart.

I decided to buy the painting, and enthusiastically showed it to our tour group when we returned to our hotel. Our Jordanian guide took one look at it, and said, "Hmph! The Miserables!" Obviously, his taste in paintings was different than mine! Yet the name he gave my painting captured the meaning it had for me.

I have the painting hanging in my bedroom now, beneath a handmade wooden cross that was a gift from a friend. Each time I walk past it, I am reminded of all the people in the world who are suffering from famine, drought, genocide, war, AIDS and other diseases, crime, inadequate housing…the list goes on and on. "The Miserables" are counting on us to help, and each time we let them down, we drive another nail into the cross of Jesus Christ, who suffers with them.

Prayer: *Forgive us, God, when we ignore the needs of others to satisfy our own. Help us listen to their cries, and find it in our heart to give what we are able to ease their suffering and bring them joy. Amen.*

An Extra Place at the Table

Do not neglect to do good and to share what you have, for such sacrifices are pleasing to God. (Hebrews 13:16)

Be hospitable to one another without complaining. Like good stewards of the manifold grace of God, serve one another with whatever gift each of you has received. (1 Peter 4:9-10)

My son Philip is a member of Rotary International, and his local club has sponsored STRIVE, a mentoring program for at-risk high school seniors. For some time, he and five or six other Rotarians have met monthly with these students for lunch and discussion. Usually they have focused on such topics as goal-setting, study habits, post-high school training opportunities, and career options.

However, one December the STRIVE mentors and students talked about how special holidays like Christmas had different meaning for people, depending on their personal situations. They shared stories of friends or family members who would not be at their family's holiday tables because of a terminal illness, a drive-by shooting, accidental death, rehab treatment, divorce, or broken relationships. Then they held hands in a circle and paused to remember in silence all those who were struggling with the painful absence of these loved ones.

Before the group left, Philip suggested that each STRIVE member set an extra place at their holiday tables to remind them not just of their absent loved ones, but of all the others who would have no chance to celebrate the holiday with their families: the homeless and hungry, the abused and neglected, the incarcerated, the hospitalized, the elderly living alone, and the workers who would be on the job to keep us safe and healthy. We are all one family, he said, and we need to find ways to care for one another.

So, let us each set an extra place at our holiday tables this year, but let's make sure this place is filled by someone in need by the time we sit down to our meal!

Prayer: *Incarnate God, make us your hands*
to wipe away sad tears,
your arms to welcome those in need,
to calm their anxious fears;
your voice to whisper angel-songs,
your smile to light their way,
until a lonely Christmas Eve
becomes glad Christmas Day.[1]

---

1. *This is the last stanza of "On Christmas Eve We Celebrate," a hymn text included in* The Song Lingers On: New Hymns for Our Journey of Faith, *Texts by Mary Nelson Keithahn and Music by John D. Horman. © Zimbel Press, 2003. Used by permission.*

Fear Not

There is no fear in love, but perfect love casts out fear. (1 John 4:18a)

After reading Dr. Seuss for the first time, I was hooked! I found his fanciful stories, odd assortment of characters, and whimsical rhymes captivating, and his insights into human life and relationships wise and wonderful.

Take, for example, "What Was I Scared Of?"[1] In this story, a young boy goes for a walk in the woods and encounters "a pair of pale green pants with nobody inside them." This strange apparition seems to follow him everywhere. The pants ride by on a bike in Grin-itch when he goes there on an errand. They row a boat past him when he is fishing on Roover River. The little boy is so scared of the spooky pants that he spends the night hiding in a brickle bush. But the next night he has an errand in the Snide field, and there he meets the pale green pants face to face. Terrified, he screams for help, until he hears the empty pants crying too. He realizes then that he is just as strange to them as they are strange to him. Compassion overcomes his fear. He sits down beside the pale green pants, puts his arm around their waist, and comforts them. From that day on, whenever the little boy and the pale green pants meet they say "Hi," because now they are friends, and neither is lonely or scared anymore.

We live in a time when we are more conscious of the differences that separate us than our common humanity as children of God. How many problems would be resolved if we could overcome our fear of people who are "different" and offer them our compassion and friendship instead!

Prayer: *God, forgive us when we avoid or exclude the strangers among us because we are afraid of anyone who is "different." Take away our fear, and fill us with compassion, so that we may treat one another as friends. Amen.*

1. From The Sneetches and Other Stories, *written and illustrated by Dr. Seuss. Random House, 1961.*

Walls or Bridges

There is no longer Jew or Greek, there is no longer slave or free, there is no longer male or female; for all of you are one in Christ Jesus. (Galatians 3:28)

The setting for a play called *Construction*[1] is a bare stage with crates, lumber, bags of cement, and tools piled about. Except for the acting area, the stage is dimly lit in order to create the illusion of empty space. The time and place are generic.

An odd assortment of people with different backgrounds and personalities enter. They have not met before, and all they have in common is their feeling that whoever put them in this place must have had a purpose. From the materials lying about, they conclude they are supposed to build something. Since there are no blueprints to be found, they start discussing what they should build. A swimming pool? A hospital? A community center? A church for their kind? Finally one person observes that, from the sounds around them, there must be people out there in the dark. Perhaps they should build a wall to protect them against these outsiders. They might be dangerous! After much discussion the others agree and they start building a wall.

Suddenly a stranger appears. Frightened, most of the builders leave, all except one young woman who remains to greet him. The stranger, carrying blueprints, explains that he has brought plans for a bridge that will connect them to people outside their little world. He urges them to tear down the wall they have built and construct this bridge instead. The others gradually return to hear him talk of love, good will, and concern for others, but the fear and suspicion that caused them to build the wall overcomes them, and they reject the stranger and his plans. As he turns to leave, they rush at him, grab him and knock him down, and then drag him to the place where a cross is lying. They put the stranger on the cross and quickly raise it up so all can see that Love has been crucified again.

At this writing, the polarization in churches and in our nation has built walls of misunderstanding, fear, rejection, and exclusion among people of different ethnic backgrounds, gender identities, moral perspectives, age groups, and theologies. How much we need a stranger to come with blueprints for tearing down these walls, and building bridges of love, faith, and hope instead!

Prayer: *God of love and understanding, come and break down the walls that divide us, that we may live with one another in peace. Amen.*

Once to Every Man and Nation

Choose this day whom you will serve.....As for me and my household,
we will serve the Lord. (Joshua 24:15, sel.)

James Russell Lowell's hymn text may no longer be politically
correct, but it still challenges us today:

> *Once to every man and nation comes the moment to decide,*
> *in the strife of truth with falsehood, for the good or evil side;*
> *some great cause, God's new messiah, offering each the*
> *bloom or blight,*
> *and the choice goes by forever 'twixt that darkness*
> *and the light.*[1]

When Adolph Hitler and the Nazi party rose to power in Germany
and began committing all kinds of atrocities, the cultured
and educated German people were strangely silent. Even the
institutional Roman Catholic and Evangelical Lutheran churches
could not find their voices to protest. Only a few spoke out, and they
paid dearly for it. One was a Lutheran pastor, Dietrich Bonhoeffer,
who seized the moment and decided to join in a plot to assassinate
Hitler. The plot failed, and Bonhoeffer was sent to a concentration
camp where he was executed shortly before it was liberated at the
war's end.

Albrecht Haushofer, a courageous professor from the University
of Berlin who had once served as an advisor to Rudolf Hess on

foreign affairs, was also arrested by the Gestapo and executed for his part in the failed plot. Although the SS guards were required to get a confession from prisoners before they were hanged or shot, Haushofer refused to comply. When the guards removed his body, however, a piece of paper dropped from his pocket. It was one of several sonnets he had written in prison. Entitled "Guilt," it read as follows:

> I am guilty,
> but not in the way you think.
> I should have earlier recognized my duty;
> I should have more sharply called evil evil;
> I reined in my judgment too long,
> I did warn,
> but not enough, and clear;
> and today I know what I was guilty of.[2]

Edmund Burke once said, "All that is necessary for the triumph of evil is that good men do nothing." When will we learn that lesson?

Prayer: *God, help us know when it is time to speak out for justice, and give us the courage to act on our words. Amen.*

---

1. *This is the first stanza of James Russell Lowell's hymn, "Once to Every Man and Nation," as it appears in the* Pilgrim Hymnal *(Pilgrim Press, 1958) set to the tune EBENEZER (TON-Y-BOTEL).*

2. *One of eighty sonnets in a collection,* Moabit Sonnets, *by Albrecht Haushofer (Athol Books, 2001). Originally published in 1946 after his death in Berlin's Moabit Prison.*

The Courage to Say No

Choose this day whom you will serve. (Joshua 24:15)

When my son Stephen and I went to Germany and Austria in 1989, we spent a few days with friends who lived in the village of Rossdorf, near Darmstadt in the Frankfurt area. Dietmar, a professor at the University of Darmstadt, and his wife Gitta were born during World War II. As children, they had lived through its terrible results, yet they knew little about its causes. Their history books in school had stopped with the year 1930. That is why, on this particular night, Dietmar had to talk. We had gathered at a little restaurant for coffee and dessert. The rest of us had been to the opera house in Darmstadt for a glorious performance of *Aida*, but Dietmar had gone to his Rotary Club meeting. The speaker had been a veteran military general from World War II, and for the first time, Dietmar had heard someone from his parents' generation talk about what he called "that damn stupid war."

"We Germans need to admit and accept responsibilities for the war and the actions of the Nazis, rather than trying to hide what they did," the general had said. "Military officers like me should have openly opposed Hitler's plans. We knew his policies were wrong, and after Stalingrad and the multiple fronts he opened, we knew the war could not be won. It was difficult to stand up to him, however. After World War I, Hitler's economic policies had worked at first, so people looked upon him as their savior. His military techniques like the blitzkrieg should not have worked, but they were successful, and it was hard to argue with success."

"This was no excuse," the general had admitted. "People just looked the other way and did not speak up. This was especially true in the case of the Jews. At first the Jews were moved away from friends and neighbors in little towns like Rossdorf into the cities, and people were told they would be happier 'with their kind.' Then in the anonymity of the cities, they were shipped off from the ghettoes to the concentration camps, along with any others Hitler wanted to get rid of. Again, few spoke up to say 'No.' Anyone who openly opposed Hitler ended up in the concentration camps too."

As Dietmar talked that evening, I thought again of these lines from a hymn:

> *Once to every man and nation comes the moment to decide*
> *In the strife of truth with falsehood, for the good or evil side.*
> (James Russell Lowell)

And today, years later, I wonder, is there a lesson in the general's story for us in our country too?

Prayer: *God, give us the courage to say "No" to what we know is wrong and evil, and "Yes" to what we know is right and good, no matter what the cost. Amen.*

A Wise Mother

Blessed are the peacemakers, for they will be called children of God.
(Matthew 5:9)

I have often wondered what the world would be like if women were in charge of nations, instead of men. Mothers do not like to send their children off to war!

That is the theme of Anita Lobel's story of a woman who lived in a valley between two countries that were at war.[1] The woman built a wall around her house to protect her two sons, a cow, some chickens, and her large potato field from the war. When the boys questioned the need for the wall, she told them it protected their potatoes from the winds from the East and the West. The family was safe and warm, and had plenty to eat.

When the boys grew up, however, they were tired of planting and weeding potatoes. The older son saw soldiers from the East marching by and ran off to join them. The next day the younger son joined a group of soldiers from the West. Their mother cried bitterly, bolted her door, and went back to her potato field.

For a while, her sons liked being soldiers, and they each became leaders of their troops. But as the battles raged on, they began thinking of potatoes and warm fires and their mother at home, and they felt sad. Soon the land was barren from the fighting, and the soldiers on both sides were starving. The sons knew where there was food, and both armies marched toward the valley where their mother lived, demanding that she give them some of her potatoes. She answered their request with silence, so both armies attacked the wall around her home. The wall came down, the house was ruined, the cow and chickens were gone, and the woman lay still on the ground. Her sons began to weep, and soon all the soldiers were weeping too, thinking of their own mothers and the destruction war brings. The mother let everyone weep for a while, and then stirred. She offered to feed them from potatoes stored in her basement, but only if they would promise to stop fighting, clean up the mess, and go home. They promised, begging her forgiveness. After a good meal and some songs, they went home to their mothers in the East and the West, took off their uniforms, and stopped making weapons. The two sons buried their swords and medals, rebuilt their mother's house, mended what was broken, and planted new potatoes in the field. But they did not rebuild the wall.

Prayer: *In a world torn by conflicts and violence, God, show us how to be makers of peace. Help us always remember that, no matter what side we are on, we are all your children, and you love us, each and every one. Help us see one another as sisters and brothers, and treat one another as friends. Amen.*

---

1. Potatoes, Potatoes, *by Anita Lobel (Harper & Row, 1967).*

Embracing the Light

Blessed Are the Peacemakers

Blessed are the peacemakers, for they will be called children of God.
(Matthew 5:9)

Sometime in the early 1980s when we lived in Minnesota, St. John's University in Collegeville offered a weekly class for area pastors in the social dynamics of religion. My husband enrolled, and I attended the last class session with him. I have always remembered one point the professor made: Finding an outside entity to hate unifies the members of any group.

That depressing observation sounded logical to me. Once the Cold War was ended and we no longer had an identifiable enemy to fear and hate, our unity as a nation began to dissolve. In our various areas of life, we began to unite against those who disagreed with our views in order to protect our own interests in every way possible. We see the end results today in the gridlock in the U.S. Congress, political extremism, a decline in ecumenical cooperation, and growing gulfs among even the closest family members over many issues.

When we served our church in Minnesota, we had two members who had strong political views. Max was a Republican and Howard a Democrat, and they never wavered in their positions. They could not agree on issues, yet they saw one another as respected opponents, not enemies, and they were the best of friends socially and in the church. How can we recover their spirit of good will in today's polarized world? Perhaps this incident can give us a clue:

In the mining town of South Pass City in Wyoming Territory, on September 2, 1869, the day before the territory's first election, Esther Morris, aged fifty-five, hosted a tea party for Republican and Democratic candidates for the Senate. She had one purpose in mind: to assure that candidates from both parties would promise that whoever won would see that women were given the right to vote and hold office in the territory. Morris made this request at a time when there wasn't a place in the world where women could vote or hold public office, yet the senatorial candidates, admiring her courage and respecting her views, promised their support. When the first territorial legislature met, all the senators were Democrats. They passed a bill that gave women the right to vote and hold office, and despite opposition from many others, the Republican governor of the territory signed the bill into law on December 10, 1869.

Esther Morris took it upon herself to bring people of different views together to work for a common good, not against a common enemy. In so doing, she gave impetus to the Nineteenth Amendment to the US Constitution that became law in August 1920, giving all women the right to vote.

Prayer: *God, give us more peacemakers like Esther Morris, and let us each be one of them. Amen.*

True Friends

A friend loves at all times, and kinsfolk are born to share adversity....
Some friends play at friendship, but a true friend sticks closer than
one's nearest kin. (Proverbs 17:17; 18:24)

In one of his last talks with his disciples (John 15:12-15), Jesus asked them to think of themselves as friends, rather than servants. Servants do not know what the master expects of them, but as friends of Jesus they know that God intends for them to love one another. I suspect the disciples spent the rest of their lives trying to figure out their roles as "friends."

Dennis Nolan's picture book story of an old fable[1] gives us some insights into the meaning of friendship. In this tale, a slave named Androcles decides to risk life on the Egyptian desert rather than suffer any more abuse as a slave. He slips away and walks across the hot sand. By the third day, his food and water are gone, and he is exhausted. Luckily, he finds a large cave with a spring of fresh water. A perfect place to hide—except that an enormous lion has found it first! Androcles is afraid, thinking he has met his end, but the lion does not attack him. He creeps closer, and hears the huge beast moan. Androcles sees that the lion has a great thorn in his paw. Forgetting his fear, he reaches over and pulls out the thorn. The lion licks his face in gratitude and soon they are curled up together in the cave, fast asleep. The next day, and for many thereafter, the lion hunts and brings food to Androcles, and Androcles is a companion for him.

Three years later, however, Roman soldiers find Androcles napping on the cliffs. They return him to his master, who tells them to throw him to the beasts. Androcles is taken to the great amphitheater in Rome, and led into the arena to face the hungry animals. At a sign from the emperor, a lion roars toward him. Androcles braces himself for the attack, but the lion stops short. Man and beast recognize each other and share a joyful greeting. When Androcles explains his friendship with the lion, the emperor lets the crowd vote to set him free. Androcles and the lion remain friends forever.

Prayer: *God, help us to be the kind of people who can make friends out of enemies, and give us compassion enough to be faithful to that friendship in times of adversity and danger. Amen.*

---

1. Androcles and the Lion, by Dennis Nolan (Harcourt Brace & Company, 1997). Nolan notes that this fable was written about CE 40 by Apion, an Egyptian who lived in Rome during the reign of Tiberius, and witnessed an incident at the Circus Maximus when a lion really did spare the life of a slave. The story has been retold through the centuries, even though the original has been lost.

Embracing the Light

A Vision of Peace

The wolf shall live with the lamb, the leopard shall lie down with the kid, the calf and the lion and the fatling together, and a little child shall lead them. The cow and the bear shall graze, their young shall lie down together; and the lion shall eat straw like the ox. The nursing child shall play over the hole of the asp, and the weaned child shall put its hand on the adder's den. They will not hurt or destroy on all my holy mountain; for the earth will be full of the knowledge of the Lord as the waters cover the sea. (Isaiah 11:6-9)

Much to my surprise, my genealogical research on my family has turned up Quaker ancestors who were contemporaries of William Penn. Perhaps that's why I have always been intrigued by the many versions of a painting called *The Peaceable Kingdom*. The artist, Edward Hicks, lived in Bucks County, Pennsylvania from 1780 to 1849. After a rather wild youth, he started attending Quaker meetings, was accepted as a member of the Society of Friends, and became one of its itinerant ministers. Hicks was also a painter who specialized in decorating coaches, household objects, and farm equipment as well as tavern signs, work that was not appreciated by some of his plain Quaker neighbors. He tried farming instead to support himself and his wife and growing family, but was unsuccessful and finally turned back to his decorative painting. However, from about 1820 to his death in 1849, Hicks also painted over sixty versions of the prophet Isaiah's vision of what peace would be like when God's rule began.

Although the details are different, Hicks used the same compositional structure in each painting. On the right, there are the animals mentioned by Isaiah, animals that should be predators and prey living together peacefully, with a little child among them. In the background at the left, Hicks included a scene of William Penn's treaty with the native Americans, adapted from a popular painting by Benjamin West. Each painting expresses Hicks' simple faith and hope that humans and animals can someday live and work together in peace, just as Isaiah had envisioned.

It is the faith and hope of this 19th century American folk artist that intrigues me every time I see one of the versions of *The Peaceable Kingdom*. He obviously saw a parallel between William Penn's treaty and Isaiah's vision. Treaties require partners to recognize and respect one another's rights, and honor agreements once they are made. That is what is needed for people of different backgrounds to live together peacefully as a community.

Prayer: *God, pour your light and love into the minds and hearts of people of all nations, that we may support efforts for making peace, instead of war, and find the courage and will to work together to make the visions of Isaiah, William Penn, and Edward Hicks a reality. Amen.*

You Can't Hide from God

They heard the sound of the Lord God walking in the garden at the time of the evening breeze, and the man and his wife hid themselves from the presence of the Lord God among the trees of the garden. But the Lord God called to the man, and said to him, "Where are you?" He said, "I heard the sound of you in the garden, and I was afraid, because I was naked; and I hid myself." (Genesis 3:8-10)

My son Philip was around four when I took him and his younger sister with me to shop for groceries in the small Montana town where we lived. As usual, Philip was wearing his beloved cowboy boots and had a cowboy hat on his head. The shopkeeper greeted us warmly. He was a member of our congregation, and the children both loved him dearly.

We filled up our cart, paid for our purchases at the check-out, and came home. As I was putting the food away, I saw Philip take off his cowboy hat and remove a package of gum from under his hat. "Why, Philip," I asked, "Where did you get that gum?" I knew I had not paid for it.

Philip looked guilty. "The storekeeper gave it to me," he explained. "I think I should call and ask him about it," I said. Philip turned away, saying, "I think I'll go hide."

My suspicions confirmed, I loaded the children back up into the car and returned to the store. His sister and I stood next to Philip when he returned the package of gum to the storekeeper and apologized for taking it. The storekeeper accepted the gum with a gentle smile and said, "Philip, if I had known you wanted that gum, I would have given it to you."

How foolish we are to live with guilt after we have succumbed to temptation! God knows all our secret transgressions, and waits for us to return with repentant hearts to be lovingly forgiven.

Prayer: *God, who knows the secrets of our hearts, forgive us when we stray and redeem us with your steadfast love. Amen.*

Be Reconciled

So when you are offering your gift at the altar, if you remember that your brother or sister has something against you, leave your gift there before the altar and go; first be reconciled to your brother or sister, and then come and offer your gift. (Matthew 5:23-24)

Dick Fagan, a friend who was an agricultural missionary in the Philippines once told our children this story:

There was a church in the Philippines where people from throughout the jungle came to worship. Life in the jungle was hard. Stealing and fighting were common. People thought they had to protect themselves. Every Sunday when they walked through the thick, tropical forest, they carried their spears at their sides.

One Sunday, during the service of worship, the minister said: "All of you who love the Lord and are treating your neighbors with love and kindness can come to this table and share in the bread and wine of the Lord's Supper." The minister waited, but not one person came forward. Puzzled, he asked, "Why won't you come to the Lord's table?"

A man stood up and said, "I do not like Juan, for he took my horse last year. He does not like Maria because her pig ruined his garden." And so it went, from one person to the next.

The minister said to the people, "Forgive one another, and then come to worship."

The people felt ashamed. One by one, they spoke quietly to those who had hurt them or made them angry, and took their hands. Then with happy faces they all came forward for the Holy Communion.

Each Sunday, from that time on, the people came through the jungle with songs, not spears. They were no longer angry or afraid. They had said they were sorry for the wrongs they had done, and had forgiven one another. Now they were ready to celebrate God's forgiveness and love. They were ready to come to the Lord's table together. Reconciliation had taken place.

Prayer: *Forgive us, God, when we arm ourselves with hurt feelings, angry words, and jealous hearts that separate us, one from the other. Help us to lay down our defenses, confess our sorrow at our actions, and offer one another hands of love and forgiveness as we gather at Christ's table in his name. Amen.*

Forgiven and Forgiving

In Christ God was reconciling the world to himself, not counting their trespasses against them, and entrusting the message of reconciliation to us. (2 Corinthians 5:19)

Our family went to the Peace Gardens in Hiroshima on a Sunday afternoon in 1972. At first glance, it looked like any other park. People were everywhere, admiring the flowers, looking at the statues, and playing games in the sunshine. But soon we saw that this park was different. The bombed-out ruins of a large building cast a shadow on the happy crowd. The statues were not of famous men, but of women and children feeling the blast of the atomic bomb our country had dropped here in 1945. Instead of masterpieces of art, the museum housed the horrible relics of atomic warfare: bits of glass, pottery, and metal all melted together; remnants of the victims' clothing; photographs of plant and animal life deformed by the radiation; stone steps bearing the imprint of a man wiped out by the intense heat. Here was the ultimate result of humanity's inability to follow the rule of love. Here was what greed, fear, distrust, and hatred had produced. The fact that the bomb may have shortened the war and prevented more loss of life was no consolation. We all left the museum with hearts heavy with sadness and shame at our country's part in such destruction.

Memories do not die easily, even after over a quarter of a century. We wondered how the crowds around us felt about us Americans. Perhaps they wondered about us too, if we thought of Pearl Harbor and Bataan and Iwo Jima when we looked at them. Yet there we were, smiling, bowing, and talking with students who wanted to practice their English on us. Once bitter enemies, we were treating one another as friends, as if the horrors of war had never been between us.

This is, after all, what forgiveness and reconciliation are all about.

Prayer: *How grateful we are, God, that though we have all fallen short of being the persons you intended us to be, you accept us as we are and see us as the kind of persons we can become. Help us, in our relationships with one another, to do the same. Help us to forgive our enemies and make them our friends. Amen.*

Grace

Grace to you and peace from God our Father and the Lord Jesus Christ.
(Philippians 1:2 or Romans 1:7b)

Eleanor Estes wrote a story about Wanda Petronski, a little girl who claimed to have a hundred dresses in her closet.[1] Wanda was quiet and plain, and her family was poor. No one believed her claim. If she had a hundred dresses, why would she wear the same blue dress to school each day? The other children began teasing her. Peggy and her friends were the worst. "How many dresses do you have now, Wanda?" they would ask. "Why don't you wear some of them?" And then they would laugh, all but Maddie. She didn't want to say anything though, as she was poor too and they might tease her next.

All the girls in the class had entered drawings in a competition for the best dress design. When the day came for the winner to be announced, everyone thought it would be Peggy. However, the girls found the walls of their room covered with dress designs, each one of them different, all created by the winner, Wanda Petronski. But Wanda was not there to receive the award for her hundred dresses. Instead, the teacher read a letter from Wanda's father saying they were moving away, and Wanda would be going to another school where she would be more welcome.

Peggy and Maddie felt awful. They went to Wanda's house to tell her how sorry they were for teasing her, but they were too late. The family had already moved. They wrote her a letter, but there was no reply. Then at Christmas, Wanda wrote to their teacher: "Please keep my hundred dresses. I have a hundred new ones in my closet. I want Peggy to have the green dress, and Maddie to have the blue one. I miss you. Merry Christmas." When the girls took their drawings home, they discovered Wanda had drawn their faces on the dresses she wanted them to have. They had not deserved her friendship, but she had liked them after all.

This is the way God's grace operates. God suffers our thoughtless, selfish acts without complaint. God loves us when we least deserve that love. God offers us forgiveness before we even ask for it.

Prayer: *How much we need your amazing grace, God! And how blessed we are to receive such love! Thank you. Amen.*

---

1. The Hundred Dresses, *by Eleanor Estes (Voyager Books, reissue edition, 1974).*

Embracing the Light

Comforters and Long Johns

Now the eleven disciples went to Galilee, to the mountain to which Jesus had directed them. When they saw him, they worshiped him; but some doubted. And Jesus came and said to them, "All authority in heaven and on earth has been given to me. Go therefore and make disciples of all nations, baptizing them in the name of the Father and of the Son and of the Holy Spirit, and teaching them to obey everything that I have commanded you. And remember, I am with you always, to the end of the age." (Matthew 28:16-20)

It was cold and snowy in Minnesota one February, when my father and I headed for his winter home in Arizona for a few weeks in the sunshine. Unfortunately, that year Arizona was cooler and wetter than usual, and sunshine was hard to find. Weather reports became an important part of our daily conversations. Wherever we went, my father, who was almost ninety-three, had a hard time keeping warm. No matter how much I pleaded with him, he simply would not put on his long underwear in Arizona! I had to keep him supplied with comforters and blankets on every excursion.

This started me thinking about the things we use to keep ourselves warm, not just physically but spiritually. Some people say they come to church to be "wrapped in the warmth of God's love." Love for them is like a great, fluffy comforter enfolding them as they sit before a fire, warm and protected against the cold outside world. I am more apt to think of God's love as a suit of long underwear insulating us from the harsh cold of winter, yet enabling us to get out and set about doing God's business in the world.

I don't think God intends us to stay home in front of our fires, wrapped in our comforters and security blankets. Rather, God clothes us with love and sends us out into the world, to set it on fire with mercy, compassion, and justice. Jesus said, "Go. Make Disciples. Baptize. Teach." We can't do that wrapped in a blanket. Long underwear is definitely the order of the day!

Prayer: *God, whose love is both our comforter and our long underwear, fire us up to leave our hearths and get going on the mission you have given us. Amen.*

Embracing the Light

Rice-Christians
or Real Christians?

Why do you call me "Lord, Lord," and do not do what I tell you? I will show you what someone is like who comes to me, hears my words, and acts on them. That one is like a man building a house, who dug deeply and laid the foundation on rock; when a flood arose, the river burst against that house but could not shake it, because it had been well built. But the one who hears and does not act is like a man who built a house on the ground without a foundation. When the river burst against it, immediately it fell, and great was the ruin of that house.
(Luke 6:46-49)

The Keys of the Kingdom, by A. J. Cronin,[1] has always been one of my favorite novels. It is the story of a Scottish priest, Father Francis Chisholm, who was sent out to China as a missionary early in the twentieth century. His predecessor had glowingly described a mission compound, with a chapel and a house for the priest, and a congregation of over one thousand baptized members. Instead, when Father Chisholm arrived, he discovered the mission compound in ruins, and the only remnant of the congregation a Chinese couple that served whatever mission offered them the highest wages! Much to his dismay, Father Chisholm discovered that his predecessor had used his ample funds to pay new members for joining his church. He had baptized hundreds of people without giving them any understanding of the gospel, just to add their names to the roster he reported to the mission offices back home. The "rice-Christians" who had swelled the church rolls had disappeared as soon as the missionary priest and his money had left!

The rest of the novel tells how Father Chisholm went about bringing people back into the mission church, building his congregation not on the sands of bribery and mass conversion, but on the rocks of faith and trust, compassion and care, love and forgiveness.

Those of us in the ministry in this century are aware that there are many people who migrate from church to church in search of more and better "rice." The temptation is always there to use our resources in ways that will attract the greatest number of people to our congregations: high-tech sound and visual equipment, contemporary "pop" music, expensive entertainment for youth. Yet we also know how Jesus himself described the fruits of his labors: "the blind receive their sight, the lame walk, the lepers are cleansed, the deaf hear, the dead are raised, and the poor have good news brought to them" (Matthew 11:5). As ministers in the Body of Christ, we are charged with calling people to join us in carrying on this work of Jesus. This mission is what is demanded of "real" Christians, and it is the strong foundation that enables us to survive in this world.

Prayer: *Make us rocks of faith and mission, God, that we may be the strong, firm foundation of a church that can withstand the storms in life and carry on the work of Jesus. Amen.*

1. The Keys of the Kingdom, *by A. J. Cronin (Boston: Little, Brown and Company, 1941).*

Embracing the Light

Telling the Good News

"Therefore let the entire house of Israel know with certainty that God has made him both Lord and Messiah, this Jesus whom you crucified." Now when they heard this, they were cut to the heart and said to Peter and to the other apostles, "Brothers, what should we do?" Peter said to them, "Repent, and be baptized every one of you in the name of Jesus Christ…For the promise is for you, for your children, and for all who are far away, everyone whom the Lord our God calls to him."
(Acts 2:36-39, sel.)

As a boy in India, Sundar Singh[1] had no use for Christians and spent hours arguing with them. Still, his wealthy Sikh father insisted that he attend the mission school. "The Christians are good people," he said. "They can teach you many things. Learn from them, and ignore their faith." But Sundar could not ignore the religion of the Christians. He finally decided to accept their Lord. His father was so angry that he threw him out of the house. Sundar, once rich, found himself a penniless Christian student.

Undismayed, Sundar chose the life of a "Sadhu" or wandering holy man, and set out to be a missionary among his people. Instead of working in a church, he traveled around the country telling all he met about the love of God in Christ.

One evening, as he was meeting with a small group in a Tibetan village, they heard heavy footsteps outside. The villagers looked at one another in terror. "It's the bandits," one whispered. "They'll kill you," another warned the holy man. But Sundar walked to the door and opened it. "Come in, my friends," he said to the bandits. "Everyone is welcome to hear the story of Jesus." The fierce-looking men nodded. "We've heard of you. We want to hear the strange stories you tell."

The nervous villagers made room for the bandits, and Sundar began again. He told how Jesus had hated wrongdoing, but was ready to forgive those who were sorry for the evil things they had one. He told how Jesus had said God wanted people to love and serve one another. He talked for a long time as the bandits listened uncomfortably. When Sundar had finished, the men left quietly, stealing nothing and harming no one.

Some who heard Sundar's stories about Jesus became Christians. We don't know if the bandits were among them. However, on the night they heard the Gospel, they acted as persons of good will and left in peace.

Prayer: *God, we give thanks for power of the Gospel to move our hearts and change our behavior, whether for one night or forever. Bless all tellers of the good news, and all who listen and respond to your love. Amen.*

1. *This story of Sundar Singh was adapted from* Stories for School Prayers, *by Eileen Scott (London: National Society S.P.C.K., 1962).*

Embracing the Light

A Lesson Learned

In those days when there was again a great crowd without anything to eat, [Jesus] called his disciples and said to them, "I have compassion for the crowd, because they have been with me now for three days and have nothing to eat. If I send them away hungry to their homes, they will faint on the way—and some of them have come from a great distance." (Mark 8:1-3)

In June 2003, I went with a group from my church in Rapid City, South Dakota, to share in the life of our sister congregation in Los Guidos, Costa Rica. The church, in a squatters' village outside of San Jose, serves refugee families from neighboring Central American countries. The church's ministry includes feeding programs for children, medical clinics, and social services as well as the usual worship, education, and social activities. Several members from our church go to Costa Rica each January to help with vacation Bible school, and for several years we have sent a larger delegation to help with work projects, share in activities for youth and children, and participate in the general life of the church.

One of the activities during our ten-day visit was a "paseo," a day's outing for several busloads of children and youth. That year we went up into the mountains to a YMCA camp. In the hope of returning with all the people we brought, we had red bandanas for everyone to wear. We organized our church delegation so each one would be responsible for a small group, and had various outdoor games planned to keep them occupied. We all knew what we were going to do as leaders. We forgot that this might not be what this group of children and youth would need! As they tumbled out of the bus and saw that wide expanse of trees and green grass, they were like colts let out to pasture! These children who were used to playing on city streets saw no need for organized games! They rolled down the grassy hillsides, climbed trees, hiked the trails, and waded in the creek (improvising swim suits from their bandanas!) Eventually they played soccer, jumped rope, watched some magic acts, ate lunch, and gathered for songs and worship. Then they all climbed back on the bus, exhausted, for the trip home, and we, wiser for the day's experiences, joined them.

Prayer: *Forgive us, God, for the many times we, as leaders in the church, have been more concerned with imposing our program agendas on our people, than letting their needs determine where we put our energies and efforts. Help us to be more like Jesus, who never let his need to preach and teach take precedence over his compassionate concern for the needs of the people he encountered. Amen.*

The Right Objective

Then Jesus said…, "Someone gave a great dinner and invited many. At the time for dinner he sent his slave to say to those who had been invited, 'Come; for everything is ready now.' But they all alike began to make excuses….Then the owner of the house…said to his slave, 'Go out at once into the streets and lanes of the town and bring in the poor, the crippled, the blind, and the lame.'" (Luke 14:16-22, sel.)

During the eighteen years we served a church in Minnesota, I directed the choir for children and youth. At Christmastime we recruited parents to drive us around town so we could sing carols for our elderly members living at the local nursing home or shut in at home. We left boxes of homemade cookies at each place where we sang. Refreshments at the church followed the caroling.

One year we went to sing carols for Bill, an elderly man who lived in one room above a downtown store not far from the church. More men, due to a variety of circumstances, lived in the other single rooms along the dingy, dimly lit hall that had one rest room and water tap at its end. Bill came out into the hall when we knocked on his door, and as the choir began to sing, the other men came out too, one by one, to listen. The youth saw them eyeing the small box of cookies they gave Bill, and wished they had more left to share. But this was the last stop and all the boxes were gone.

When we gathered back at the church, we processed what we had just experienced. No one in the choir had been in the rooming house before, and they were shocked by the dreary, lonely existence of these men. They resolved that next year when they caroled, they would bring cookies for every man on the floor. They also decided to make Christmas stockings for each of the men, and fill them with small gifts. They carried out their plans and even took treats and cards to the men at Easter and other holidays.

Finally the choir youth asked their parents to help them cook a special holiday meal at the church, and they sent invitations to all the men in the rooming house to come. On the appointed day, they prepared the food, set a beautiful table, and eagerly awaited their guests. But the only one who came was the man who belonged to the church. "The others are not comfortable coming to a meal in church," he said. "They never go to church. They wouldn't know how to act."

The youth were crushed. "But we worked so hard on this," they said. Then they looked at one another, and all the food they had prepared, and declared, "Then we'll take our dinner to them." And that's just what they did, much to the delight of their reluctant but hungry guests.

Prayer: *God, may we always accept people as they are, and seek to understand their needs, not ours, when we offer our help. Amen.*

A Wise and Generous Gift

Those who are generous are blessed, for they share their bread with the poor. (Proverbs 22:9)

Several years ago, when the AIDS epidemic was raging in Africa, missionaries from the Congo spoke to the Sunday School at Warner Presbyterian Church in Kensington, Maryland.

"The AIDS epidemic is taking a terrible toll on human lives in our country," they said. "We should be providing AIDS prevention education for our young people, but it is so difficult to get children and youth to come to our churches for any reason. The young people love playing soccer, but they have to improvise their own equipment. Their soccer balls are whatever materials they can bunch together, wrapped with duct tape. If you want to help us reach these youth, send us some soccer balls."

That sounded like a good idea to Jan Moody, director of Christian education at the church. She shared the missionaries' request with the manager of a supply store that outfitted the many soccer teams in their suburban area. The manager pointed to some orange soccer balls. "I could give you those," he said. "No one is buying balls in that color. I'll see if my district manager will approve."

The next day, when Jan went back to give the manager a mailing address for the missionaries, he told her, "My district manager thinks this is a great idea. There's no market here for these orange soccer balls. We'll supply you with 800, and mail them to the Congo at our expense!"

A year later, every church related to the Presbyterian mission in the Congo had a soccer team, and there were soccer leagues all over the area. And each practice started with AIDS prevention education for the young athletes!

Those who are generous are blessed, and become a blessing to others!

Prayer: *God, may we too be wise and generous in responding to the needs of your children, wherever they may be. Amen.*

Christian Missions:
A Two-Way Street

Now you are the body of Christ and individually members of it. And God has appointed in the church first apostles, second prophets, third teachers; then deeds of power, then gifts of healing, forms of assistance, forms of leadership, various kinds of tongues.
(1 Corinthians 12:27-28)

Growing up during World War II and its aftermath, I was aware of the tremendous need for relief and reconstruction in Europe and Asia. I had been corresponding with about fifty pen pals, and our family had sent CARE packages to some of them who lived in Europe. Our offerings at church went to work in other areas. It was not surprising that my concept of Christian mission work in those years was "helping those poor people over there."

Our family's trip to Japan in 1972 challenged this idea. By this time, Japan's standard of living was not so different from our own, and I questioned if and why there was still a need for foreign missionaries there. Our missionary friends pointed out that Christians had more than material aid to offer the Japanese people. We had this "higher law" that could help them discover the power of forgiveness, find meaning in suffering, and experience a sense of community that was not part of the Japanese culture. Moreover, said our friends, Japanese Christians had gifts of faith to offer us that were unique, and, indeed, some of them were now coming to this country as missionaries to us!

Our visit to Japan helped us learn that Christian missionary work was never a one-way street. We are all "those poor people over there," as well as those who come "bearing gifts."

Prayer: *Give us humble hearts, God, when we interact with Christians from other cultures. Help us to honor and respect the gifts of faith they offer us, even as we seek to share our gifts of faith with them. Amen.*

The Unknown Scout of Japan

But I say to you that listen, Love your enemies, do good to those who hate you.…Do to others as you would have them do to you.
(Luke 6:27, 31)

My son Philip, an Eagle Scout and experienced Scoutmaster, has shepherded local and regional troops to several national and world jamborees where he has had opportunities to meet Scouts from many different cultures and countries. When he returned from the 2015 World Scout Jamboree in Yamaguchi, Japan, he described a visit the Scouts had made to a memorial in the Kodomonokuni Children's Theme Park in Yokohama. The memorial is a metal relief in a rock-walled recess in a hillside. The relief shows a Japanese soldier tending a wounded American solider lying on the ground with his hand on his chest in a three-fingered Scout salute. A metal sculpture of another Scout stands to one side of the relief, saluting the two men.

It seems that during World War II, on one of the small islands in the South Pacific, American marines and Japanese soldiers had engaged in a fierce battle. One marine was left behind by his comrades who did not see that he had been injured. The marine's foot was bleeding and he soon lost consciousness. When he awoke, he heard Japanese soldiers moving in the near-by brush and gasped. The sound caught the attention of a solider about his age. He was wearing a grass-covered helmet and carried a rifle with a long bayonet. The marine sighed. *I'm going to die*, he thought to himself, as the soldier moved toward him. He heard the Japanese soldier cock his rifle, and covered his face with his hand as he passed out again. Sometime later, when it was dark, the marine regained consciousness and marveled that he was still alive. Curiously his foot had been bandaged and was no longer bleeding! When his comrades came back to find him, the marine saw a piece of paper on a nearby branch and put it in his pocket. Later, when he was at the field hospital, he took it out and read:

> When I went to kill you with my bayonet, you unconsciously saluted me with three fingers, and I understood that you were a brother Scout. I was a Scout in Japan and I cannot kill my Scout brother. You fought bravely against my unit and were wounded. Soldiers who are wounded become non-combatants according to our Samurai code of honor. I bound up your wound. I am sorry I didn't have better medicines. Good luck. In better times we might have met at a World Jamboree.

After the war, the marine returned home with this story, and a few years later a national Scout leader told it to Japanese Scout leaders at an international meeting. The Japanese soldier who had spared the marine was never found, but Scouts from all over Japan honored him by contributing to the cost of the memorial that honored this Unknown Scout.

Prayer: *God of peace and good will, help us to look upon all your children as our brothers and sisters that we may meet one another in world jamborees instead of in war. Amen.*

The Second Mile

And if anyone forces you to go one mile, go also the second mile.
(Matthew 5:41)

When our family of six was traveling in Japan in 1972, we went mostly by train. Coming from a small town in Minnesota, we were amazed at the huge number of people that passed through Japanese train stations night and day. Everywhere we looked, people were rushing to catch a train to work, to school, to play, to visit friends. The train stations were a maze of corridors, stairways, and platforms. Most of the signs were written in Japanese characters, and few of the workers spoke English.

On this particular day, we got off the famous bullet train in Nagoya, and looked for the subway that would take us out to a ferry in the harbor. We found ourselves hopelessly confused. Finally, we showed our ferry tickets to a young Japanese businessman. He did not speak English, but motioned for us to wait while he asked directions at a newsstand. Then he showed us where to buy our train tickets, bought one for himself, and led us to the proper train. He rode with us long enough to help us transfer to the subway that would take us out to the ferry. Then, bowing with a smile, he disappeared into the crowd.

Our church back home had always had a "Second Mile Mission," but this was the first time I really understood what it meant to give above and beyond what was asked. The kind young man had known that words alone would not be enough to help us find our way. He had to "go the second mile" and come with us to get us on the right train.

Prayer: *God, you went the second mile when you came to us in Jesus. You too knew that words were not enough to show us the way to go, the way of love. Thank you. Amen.*